Beyond the Script

Beyond the Script
Drama in the Classroom

Robyn Cusworth

Jennifer Simons

 Primary English Teaching Association

Copying for Educational Purposes
The Australian *Copyright Act* 1968 allows a maximum of one chapter or 10% of this book, whichever is the greater, to be copied by any educational institution for its educational purposes provided that that educational institution (or the body that administers it) has given a remuneration notice to Copyright Agency Limited (CAL) under the Act.

For details of the CAL licence for educational institutions contact CAL,
19/157 Liverpool Street, Sydney NSW 2000
Telephone (02) 9394 7600, Facsimile (02) 9394 7601
E-mail info@copyright.com.au

Copying for other purposes
Except as permitted under the Act, for example a fair dealing for the purposes of study, research, criticism or review, no part of this book may be reproduced, stored in a retrieval system, or transmitted in any form or by any means without prior written permission. All inquiries should be made to the publisher at the address below.

National Library of Australia Cataloguing-in-Publication data

Cusworth, Robyn Ann
Beyond the script: drama in the classroom

Bibliography
ISBN 1 875622 26 8

I. Drama in education 2. Drama - Study and teaching (Primary).
3. Drama - Study and teaching (Secondary) I. Simons, Jennifer.
II. Primary English Teaching Association (Australia). III. Title.

372.66044

Reprinted May 2000
First published November 1997
Copyright © Primary English Teaching Association 1997
Laura Street Newtown NSW 2042 Australia

Cover by MG Design
Photographs by Tanya Poole
Edited by Jeremy Steele
Typeset in Giovanni in 10.5/13.5 and Avant Garde by Katherine Stevenson
Printed by Star Printery
21 Coulson Street, Erskineville, NSW 2043

CONTENTS

Preface vii

1 What is educational drama?
   Describing educational drama 1
   Role 2
   Focus 7
   Tension 7
   Symbol 8
   Reflection and disengagement 8

2 Revisiting 'Old Faithful': drama games with a difference
   Comparing drama and games 9
   Using drama games productively 11
   Choosing the game 12
   Games during or after a drama 14

3 Movement, mime and still image: beginning in drama
   Relaxation exercises 16
   Movement 17
   Still image 18
   Mime 20

4 Exploring teacher in role and mantle of the expert
   The rationale for using teacher in role 23
   The importance of careful planning 24
   Steps in planning 25
   Some features of TIR 27
   Mantle of the expert 28

5 Programming: using literature as a starting point
   The outcomes approach and drama 30
   Bringing about change 31
   Programming drama in other key learning areas 32
   Programming drama using literature as a starting point 33

6   **Puppetry in dramatic contexts**
        Metaphor puppets and objects 37
        Types of puppets useful in the classroom 38
        Beginning with puppets in the classroom 39
        Staging a puppet play 41

7   **Playbuilding**
        The nature of playbuilding 43
        The background of playbuilding 44
        Introducing and teaching playbuilding 45

8   **Storytelling: defining who we are**
        The importance of oral storytelling 50
        The structure of stories 52
        Nurturing a sense of story in our students 52

9   **Readers' theatre: from text to script**
        Rationale for readers' theatre 57
        Adapting a literary text 59
        Starting with readers' theatre 60
        Children scripting 61

10   **Taking shape: aesthetics and drama form**
        Making and watching 63
        Role within role 63
        Protection into role 64
        From making to aesthetic understanding 64
        Creating a performance for others: acting and directing 65
        Watching others perform: the spectator function 65
        Working with a script 66

11   **Evaluation and assessment**
        Defining evaluation and assessment as terms in drama 68
        Principles of evaluation and assessment in drama 69
        Appropriate evaluation tools in drama 70

Envoi 73

Appendix: Drama programs for novels and picture books
                 Margery Hertzberg 75

Select bibliography 85

PREFACE

> You'll never really understand a person until you consider things from his point of view . . . until you climb into his skin and walk around in it.
>
> (Harper Lee, *To Kill a Mockingbird*)

This comment from Atticus to his children encapsulates what drama can do in any classroom or learning context. It enables us to step out of our own life situation into another person's. Through drama we can begin to understand how others think, feel and respond to the world, and so enlarge our understanding of ourselves. It's this element of exploration inherent in the drama process that's most important, even if the end product is a theatrical performance.

Many teachers remain tentative about using drama in their classrooms, and yet, as Gavin Bolton suggests, it can be a most powerful teaching and learning methodology across the curriculum. There's a large body of research which suggests that learners are more likely to take risks and 'have a go' at problem solving if they're working in a context where they're having fun, feel trusted and supported, and are motivated. In addition, if they're working in a fictional context, the real-life consequences of taking a risk are minimised. Educational drama meets all these requirements, but remains a Cinderella in the classroom.

We hope that this book will give teachers a feel for a number of different dramatic forms and strategies and some ideas for using them to enhance their students' learning. From the outset, however, we want to emphasise that beginning in drama is about taking risks. It's quite normal for inexperienced students to be overexcited to start with, and equally normal for there to be some initial self-consciousness all round. And if some early drama experiences lead to confusion and disarray, that's all right too. However, it is important to establish some drama 'rules' and discuss these parameters explicitly with students.

Drama challenges the old notion of the teacher as transmitter of expert knowledge. While various kinds of knowledge and skill are obviously important in drama, the best learning comes from negotiating them. In this regard, it's a great advantage for teachers to understand and make plain to their students that they are co-learners in the drama experiences which they plan and implement.

Some of the examples in this book are drawn from our own work in schools with beginning primary and secondary teachers. Further examples have been supplied by the work of teachers in other schools. To all who have helped us we extend our sincere appreciation, and we especially wish to thank:

- Margery Hertzberg, author of the Appendix and fellow-explorer of drama in education
- Tanya Poole for her photographs
- David Smith for his constructive suggestions on drafts of the manuscript
- Jeremy Steele for his careful and inspirational editing
- Vivienne Nicoll-Hatton for her encouragement and support
- all the staff and students at Curl Curl North Primary School for their involvement in the University of Sydney's drama and literacy programs, and especially Trish Cavenagh, Kerry Scott, Faye Jackson, Barbara Moxham and Jodie Stokes
- Anna Dickinson, Mirelli Farrell and Frances Zagari for permission to adapt ideas developed in their units of work
- Jill French for her careful word processing and good-natured revisions of chapters
- Kerry Walls for initial transcription of lecture material
- all our students, current and past, who've helped us to extend, adapt and develop our ideas about the use and importance of drama in the classroom.

1   WHAT IS EDUCATIONAL DRAMA?

The question 'What is drama?' is as old as Aristotle, and one that most people have an opinion about. When we asked a number of pre-service teachers for their opinions recently, responses like 'acting' were common. Some equated drama with life in turmoil, or the kind of exciting events that make newspaper headlines. Some who had had drama lessons at school suggested that the essence lay in playing fun games or 'skits'. Others who had had a different experience at school saw drama as the reading of plays or the performing of a script for an audience. While all of these ideas may be partly true, none really reflects the nature of educational drama. This chapter attempts to describe what that is, focusing on the use of drama in primary schools.

Describing educational drama

In the educational field, drama is generally seen both as a method of teaching-learning across the curriculum areas and as a body of knowledge in its own right. Essentially it's about using drama for learning, challenging and thinking about life — about enabling students to understand different viewpoints or perspectives by exploring issues, questions or ideas through dramatic forms and devices. Educational drama can be used, for example, to examine the effects of war on a society, to develop an understanding of a particular literary character's motives, or to facilitate the use of conversational language for new speakers of English. At the same time drama can extend students' understandings of creative processes.

Drama will have many different faces in the classroom; it won't always mean some children performing prepared scripts in front of others. Sometimes it will involve the whole class (and often the teacher) improvising in role together. For example, the teacher in role as a novice cleaner consults the experienced cleaners (the K–2 children) about how to clear up Cinderella's ballroom, and then begins to gossip with them about Cinderella's fate (Warren 1991, p. 61). At other times students will work in pairs or small groups, preparing and then sharing their improvisations with the whole class. Sometimes they will be very still, thinking, planning or reflecting; sometimes they will be drawing or writing in role, or researching aspects of the past in the library.

Two terms commonly used to refer to drama with an educational objective are 'drama in education' and 'process drama' (O'Neill 1995, p. xvi). The body of theory underlying drama in education has been steadily growing since the 1960s. Although there have been many shifts and reconsiderations (as befits any form of art or education), there is also a fair amount of agreement about what constitutes good drama teaching. To ensure a good drama lesson, it can be argued, the teacher needs to plan for several components: namely, **role**, **focus**, **tension** and the use of **symbol**. Each of these is introduced below and explored in more depth in later chapters.

Role

The essence of drama activity in the primary school is for the children to step into another person's shoes and explore important issues, situations, relationships and beliefs through the process of enactment. That is, they learn to take on roles which are both similar to and different from those of their real lives, temporarily adopting another person's perspective. They use their bodies to explore the consequences of thinking in this way, maintaining their stance as other students in different roles interact with them.

The teacher is often in role too, inside the fictional event with the class. She may need to demonstrate moving in and out of role, so that the students can see that sometimes she is pretending to be, say, the Wicked Witch or an advertising executive, and sometimes stepping out of role and speaking as the teacher. Students may also need to try walking around the room, coming in and out of role, so that they can play with the differences between the pretend character and themselves. Bolton (1984, p. 106) has called this 'bracketing off from living'.

Some personalities, both children and adults, can accept fiction and 'pretending' more readily than others. There is a whole range of reasons for this: for instance, some people prefer staying anchored in the 'real' world and find it quite frightening, difficult or embarrassing to move into a fictional world. Thus, when you're introducing drama, you may need to spend time allowing students to learn that adopting a role is non-threatening, and that what happens in the drama has no consequences outside it.

Moving into role

A very important concept for drama is **protection into role**. This doesn't mean avoiding emotion, but structuring the work so that students are able to explore emotions safely. If a distance is established between the students' reality and the fiction, they are saved from confusing the fictional world with distressing elements of reality. The roles they adopt should be clearly different from themselves. For example, you can move their ages up several years and spend time establishing the fictional background. You can ask them to name and draw their setting. If it's a school, it can be placed in a different part of the country so that they're not obviously talking about their real school. If the material is 'hot' (i.e. potentially threatening), then distanced, more contemplative techniques like tableaux are preferable to real-time improvisation.

What is educational drama?

Establishing a distance between the students' reality and the fiction allows them to move into role more easily. This girl belongs to a group of Kindergarten children who were asked to come dressed as pirates and show with their faces what kind of pirate they were.

Improvisation and role

Drama can be seen as a form of game-playing, and students need to understand its rules before they can participate. Not everything is planned, and one of the rules for working in role is thinking on one's feet, or what's called **improvisation**. The essence of improvisation is spontaneity. In everyday life much of what we do is fairly predictable, but when confronted by unexpected events we act spontaneously, drawing on our intuition, imagination and perhaps our past experiences of similar events. In improvisation these spontaneous reactions are harnessed and employed in 'controlled conditions to gain insight into the problems presented' (Hodgson & Richards 1972, p. 215). Students have to respond to 'offers' of action — statements with embedded suggestions of context or character that can be taken up or rejected. To do so successfully, they need to be able to pick up and elaborate on contextual cues, some of which can be very subtle.

To create roles in an improvised fictional world, students must draw on their experiences and understanding of the real world. Moreover, they need to be able to do this in real time, acting spontaneously. For example, if you say, 'Oh, Humpty Dumpty, you look a bit broken up there, what's happened to you?', the student addressed has to be able to recognise the allusion to the nursery rhyme and quickly give a matching response (e.g. 'I fell off the wall'). Depending on students' background knowledge of culture or stories, they may need to have a class discussion and pooling of ideas before improvising. However, if you're confident that they have sufficient background information, they may enjoy an abrupt leap into the drama world.

Making an offer

Drama depends on students being able to accept each other's offers in a given situation. Working in role is a collaborative exercise in which participants build a composite picture of the drama world, negotiating its reality as the characters interact and improvise. Although any participant's line of dialogue or action (i.e. any offer) may be rejected, too solid a rejection can block the drama. For example, if the offer 'You're wearing a green dress' is met with a response like 'It's not green, it's red', that could finish the drama. The students may need to be taught how to accept an offer, or how to disagree without blocking — for example, 'Oh, you think that this is green? Through my sun-glasses it looks red.' It's also possible to accept part of the offer and adjust some of the details, as in 'No, take those green-coloured glasses off — they're affecting your sight.' Improvisation will help students to work collaboratively in this way.

Levels of role

Different levels of role are used in educational drama, and it's important for students to have some understanding of them. Five levels have been distinguished by Morgan and Saxton (1987, p. 30), and they are summarised below.

1. At the first level, **dramatic playing**, students are themselves in a make-believe situation. For example, K–2 students on an imaginary trip to Old Macdonald's farm are not required to be anybody but themselves. They just have to accept the fiction of the chickens and geese and whatever else is 'found' on the farm.

2. The next level is called **mantle of the expert**. Here students speak as if they are 'the ones who know', perhaps architects who designed a new building or archaeologists who have just dug up a dinosaur bone.

3. At the third level is **role playing**, or adopting somebody else's point of view. At this level students won't be speaking with an accent, or hobbling with a crooked stick, or trying to make their bodies look other than they naturally are. The focus is *internal* — they take on the attitude of somebody else, speaking and behaving as they believe such a person would speak and behave. They may, for example, be taking the position of a logger or a conservationist in a discussion about logging Australia's forests.

4. At the fourth level students begin to represent an individual lifestyle. For example, they may be **characterising** an old lady, which is different from

role playing an old lady. In characterising, students begin to adopt signs (e.g. articles of clothing or ways of speaking) and they'll need time to explore some of the different possibilities of representing a role. So while characterising is appropriate for prepared drama like readers' theatre, it may be the wrong level for a real-time improvisation where students need to think on their feet.

5 The final level, **acting**, is where students move from classroom exploration to performing before an audience. They need to give considerable thought to things like costume, make-up, symbolic objects, talking with an accent, movement, using space and so on. The emphasis shifts from enjoying an experience for oneself to creating an experience for the spectator.

Each level of role is useful at different times. In planning a drama lesson you need to consider both the cognitive challenge involved and the abilities of the students, and your choice of objective will indicate which level is the most suitable.

Building roles

Three things are important in the building of roles: role **function**, the **status** that the role has, and the **attitude** that the role adopts towards the world. Each role has a **function** in creating the totality of the drama. Questions such as:

What is the character trying to achieve?

How does he/she assist or hinder the others?

can be asked to help students think about a particular character's role.

Sometimes the character may not get much further than a simple role function. If, for example, we're exploring 'The Bulldozer Man', we don't really care what his personal life is at home; all that's important is the fact that he's going to bulldoze the trees. Sometimes, in issues-based drama, students don't need to go much deeper than a simple role function — though this may change as the drama goes on. For instance, the Bulldozer Man might be converted and become the Environmentalist by the end.

At other times, however, **status** is important in role development, particularly when the teacher is also in role. In such cases, questions like these may need to be considered:

How much power does the character have relative to the other people in the performance?

Who is the leader?

Is he/she in danger of being overthrown in this particular group, or is this leader an almighty person that everybody's afraid of?

Is it a benevolent dictatorship?

Knowing what power the character has will affect the vocabulary, presence and tone of voice used. It will also contribute to each character's particular **attitude** (or emotional position) towards the events being considered in the drama. Questions like:

What actions are implied by the attitude?

What actions will demonstrate it?

will help students to concentrate on attitude as a way of developing a role.

Sometimes the real intentions of the role are hidden and the students are, knowingly or unknowingly, working with subtext. Just what it is may remain unclear for a while; they simply become aware that there's some sort of hidden agenda. For example, students working on 'Snow White' with the teacher in role must determine what her character really intends . . . *This old lady seems to be offering me a great gift with this golden apple, but I don't trust her shifting eyes or her tone of voice. What's she really doing?* As they become more sophisticated with role, students learn to use subtext themselves as they take on an attitude: the exploiting employer may 'smile and smile and be a villain'.

Managing and modelling roles

Once students begin to present another person's point of view, the question of stereotyping emerges. How do we know what other people would do or think? Gavin Bolton has talked about two ways of acting in real life: 'modelling' and 'managing'. **Modelling** involves basing our behaviour on what we've done in the past or what we've seen somewhere else — the behaviour of our parents, peers, movie stars, etc. Sometimes we present the character type, and this can result in drama like a TV advertisement. Stereotyping, however, is not always a bad thing; it can result in very funny work.

Managing indicates a form of behaviour that's less common in our lives. For many people, days are so predictable that they don't have to think much about what to do; they seldom have to make quick decisions that have implications for what happens next. But when you are managing, you really have to think about what you're doing. For example, if you're travelling in a foreign country, you often have to 'manage' because you can't speak the language and must think about other ways to communicate. When you suddenly encounter something for which you have no precedent, then you are out of modelling and into managing

The style of drama introduced by Dorothy Heathcote in Britain in the 1960s combined managing and modelling. One example is the 1970s videotape 'Building Belief', a role play about early American colonists. In the early stages of the lesson students used modelling, building up roles using their knowledge of historical characters until they felt comfortable. Then they were issued with a challenge which they had to deal with in a managing mode. First Heathcote had given them, as settlers, freedom to divide up the land amongst themselves. Next she angrily challenged them to defend the fact that they hadn't given any to the oldest citizen, Martha Sharp (Heathcote's character), and they had to manage relations with a distressed old lady.

Focus

Although role can be seen as the essence of drama, there are several other essential components, one of which is **focus**. A good lesson has to be planned to ensure that the work is focused, that it centres around a worthwhile educational objective (or outcome). When drama fails, it's often because it's formless or tries to cover too much. All of the great plays have a central focus — a worthwhile theme to which all the events of the play contribute. *The Merchant of Venice*, for example, looks at issues of justice and equity; *The Crucible* examines what can happen when fear overtakes rationality; *Pygmalion* explores the notions of class and language. As the teacher, you need to decide what your focus will be and how drama can help you explore this central issue.

Classroom drama can be focused by introducing what Gavin Bolton calls the 'second dimension' of role, an aspect of life that the students know from experience. For example, in a drama about bushrangers, students would probably enact a stereotype and be limited to what they know about bushrangers from film or books. But if the focus is *nervous* bushrangers, they can bring to the drama a dimension of life they have experienced themselves and so improvise more effectively. Then the kind of questions explored at a metaphorical level might be:

Do I trust my friends?

Am I a brave person?

What will I do if the thing that I'm expecting to happen is not as I expect it?

This second dimension is very important for focusing drama work, and when you set up a drama, you should be building into the roles some aspect that the students do know about. Bolton talks about the 'adjective' of the role — the children play not astronauts but *first-time* astronauts.

Tension

Another essential component in drama is **tension**. Drama examines the processes of living, which usually involve different drives or forces competing with each other. It's when the conflict is unresolved, when there's a state of tension, that drama exists. One of the Macquarie Dictionary's definitions of tension is 'intense suppressed anxiety, suspense or excitement', which helps to reflect its positive aspect. As Morgan and Saxton (1987, pp. 22–24) have suggested, it is the *excitement* which engages learners both intellectually and emotionally and motivates them to become involved in the drama activity.

Lesson planning for drama therefore needs to identify the sources of tension and maintain them. Gavin Bolton also talks about the 'art of constraint', the techniques that maintain tension by postponing the climax. For example, you could change the time-frame in which your students are operating: they could become astronauts in space, weightless and only able to walk in very slow motion. With running impossible, they need to work out a different plan for escaping space monsters. The lesson has a built-in tension, a constraint that is going to delay the climax of reaching the safety of the spaceship. Alternatively you might limit space so that the students have to crawl on hands and knees through a tunnel. This kind of constraint will set up a different kind of tension.

In a role play where characters are arguing, the constraint could be in your instructions to the students in role — for example, 'I want her to know that you're angry but you're not allowed to put it into words; you can't actually say, "I'm very angry with you".' The students have to try less direct, more ambiguous methods of communication.

Symbol

The last component of drama that must be introduced here is the use of **symbol**. Drama usually works best if the theme applies at several levels: for instance, a play about the convict era might also represent a timeless conflict between justice and loyalty. To reinforce such general metaphors, objects or events are often used repeatedly to accumulate meaning and emotional connotations. Thus, in a drama about runaways, the family photograph which the girl constantly carries can eventually stand alone to represent her longing for home.

While an object (or a word or movement) may come to have a shared meaning, you can also give students an opportunity to think about what it might symbolise for them individually. For example, an old-fashioned oil lamp placed in the centre of the class circle may symbolise warmth and hope for some students, but for others it may signify something quite different — silence and solitude perhaps.

Reflection and disengagement

In educational drama students adopt roles in order to learn about other people and themselves, and it's important for them to be given the chance to articulate that learning and compare their experiences with those of others. It's also important that they spend time disengaging from their roles, or 'de-roling', especially if their emotions have been aroused. You may need to encourage them to talk about the roles they've been playing in order to help them make a clear distinction between the fiction and reality.

2 REVISITING 'OLD FAITHFUL': DRAMA GAMES WITH A DIFFERENCE

Many teachers believe in the value of games to 'warm up' students or introduce them to some of the essential skills of drama, such as collaboration, focus and the channelling of energy. Indeed it's normal for teachers to start students quite new to drama in this way. Watching individuals as they keep (or don't keep!) to the rules of the game, as they lead, follow and/or collaborate, can be useful for diagnosing the level at which to begin drama proper. Moreover, adapting the content of a game to whatever drama theme is about to be explored can be an excellent way of easing students into the appropriate mood, or defining parameters that will help them identify the theme.

Yet while teachers find drama games useful and students obviously enjoy them, there's a danger that they can become a 'quick fix' — sufficient fun in themselves to distract students from the serious intentions of educational drama. Games can overexcite young children, and their usually fast pace often leads to a breakdown between cognitive and affective learning. Unfortunately, for some students, drama extends no further than games used as lesson breaks or to fill in before the bell. So this chapter takes a fresh look at drama games and suggests a different perspective.

Comparing drama and games

There are four main similarities between drama and games, viz:
- the need for rules
- separation from the consequences of real life
- tension
- awareness of the roles of all the people involved.

These similarities (which are discussed below) have been seen as significant in drama theory. As Peter Slade (1954) observed, young children learn primarily by play, and an understanding of what and how they learn through games can help teachers to plan for learning through drama.

The need for rules

Gavin Bolton (1987) makes the important point that drama and games both have a formal order: if the rules aren't followed, the game will break down or the drama will collapse. Most games involve allocating different role functions to the players, who then interact according to set rules. For example, in *What's the time, Mr Wolf?*, the wolf's role is to keep his back turned and only give chase after shouting 'Dinner time!' Children demonstrate their awareness of the importance of rules by expressing outrage if they are broken (e.g. if the wolf peeks). Yet, paradoxically, they will sometimes gleefully and deliberately flout the rules. For instance, they might call out the wrong formula question, the wolf might become 'Silly old Kangaroo', or the object of the game might become not to escape the wolf but to get caught. Flouting usually leads to an alternative game of 'breaking the rules', where children branch off into a parody of the original game.

The same sort of breakdown may happen in drama. Students can't create an alternative world unless they stay within an agreed paradigm. Nevertheless they sometimes choose to flout it, either overtly or covertly satirising the original intention. For example, a play about outwitting the opposition might be disrupted by a child deliberately introducing a gun. There could be many reasons for this, but most probably in setting up the drama the teacher had been unable to engage the students' interest, or they didn't understand the 'rules'. Sometimes a class equates drama with excitement, and pulling a gun reminds them of TV or the movies. Generally speaking, however, games and drama both require the observation of rules, and usually this is accompanied by a high degree of concentration or, as Peter Slade says, 'absorption'.

Separation from the consequences of real life

Drama and games are both bracketed off from real life: in each it's possible to try out alternative actions with no external consequences. Thus, in a game of *Monopoly*, one can gamble with money and property without any real loss; in a wartime drama one can play a traitor without really causing harm. This sort of bracketing off has been referred to as 'disinterested interest' — children are engaged in the action and care about what happens, but there's nothing permanent at stake.

Although drama requires a suspension of disbelief, students need to understand that even if they're operating in a fiction, they should still be aware of the real world. The drama can collapse if they don't know what is real and what is not. If they ask questions like 'Is this really happening?' or 'Are you really a witch?', it indicates that the lines between reality and the drama world are becoming blurred. Sometimes drama roles can only be maintained if students have reality signalled to them very strongly. Especially with K–2 children, you may need to wear a hat or similar symbol to show that you're in role. It's also a good idea to allow K–2 children to signal that they wish to escape the fiction if it cuts too close to their reality (e.g. 'If you put your hands on your head and wear your invisible hat, you can't be seen by the witch').

Whenever you sense the need to break the fiction, you should have the class come out of role and reflect on what's happened in the drama. It may be best to come in and out of role several times, and it's especially important to spend time reflecting and de-roling after an emotionally strong episode. Even questions like 'When you were the hostage, how did you feel about . . . ?' can help re-establish reality.

Tension
There are many sources of dramatic tension but, as mentioned in the previous chapter, what they generally have in common is that they prevent a climax from occurring: we see forces in conflict with each other but the resolution of the conflict is postponed. This is as true of games as plays. For example, in *Hamlet* the hero can't obey his father's ghost and kill his uncle until he tests the ghost's validity, until he watches his uncle's reaction to the players re-enacting the murder, until he speaks with his mother, and so on. Tension is created whilst we wait for resolution, and the tension maintains the drama. When Hamlet does kill his uncle, the drama is all but over. The same sort of thing occurs in *Hide and seek*, where the fun of the game is in the mounting tension as, one by one, the hidden players are found. As soon as all are caught, the game's over.

Role function
You can only play a game if you understand what you're doing relative to the other players. You can't be a goalkeeper in soccer unless you understand that the other team is trying to kick the ball past you into the goal and that they believe you're going to try to stop it going in. Playing the game depends on you understanding not only your own function, but theirs too. People who kick an 'own goal' aren't very popular with their own team — either they haven't understood the rules, or they haven't been able to fulfil the role function.

The same sort of thing happens in drama. If you don't really understand what the other people in a group role play are doing, you can't develop your own role. That's why students from different cultural contexts, or students learning English as a second language, may need to be given a lot of information about the social or linguistic context of the drama and a clear idea of how people usually behave and speak in that situation. If they don't understand what's expected of them relative to the others, they won't be confident about taking part.

Using drama games productively
When you're planning to use a drama game, you should be clear about the reason for introducing it. It may be as a way of easing students from one way of thinking (individual, logical) to another (collaborative, lateral), or perhaps to focus their attention when they've just left the playground after recess. It may be that you're using the game as a way of surreptitiously

mixing the students — pairing them to work with classmates who end up next to them instead of working in friendship groups.

Games are usually played at the beginning of a lesson, yet they may be more effectively placed in the middle (to increase tension) or at the end (to help de-roling). What the game is and where it's placed will depend on the objective for the whole lesson.

Choosing the game

There are many books, such as Peter Moore's *When Are We Going To Have More Drama?* (1988) and Steve Matthews' *Getting into the Act* (1988), which include collections of games that can be adapted to drama. Games can be classified by the purpose they serve in a drama lesson, and in your planning it's important to make sure that there's a clear link between the game and the other steps of the lesson.

Name games can set up a climate conducive to collaborative work, and they can be particularly useful when students don't know each other. Here are some common games, with suggestions for the next steps into drama:

1 Sitting in a circle, students call out their own names one by one. This beginning can be elaborated by adding an alliterative adjective to the name (e.g. 'Happy Hannah'), and perhaps an illustrative action (e.g. jumping in the air with arms up). A drama about different feelings might start from grouping students with similar adjectives or actions.

2 Before giving their own names, students repeat the names of all the people in the circle ahead of them. This could be followed by a discussion about memory, and a drama based on remembering lists.

3 Students call out their names and add an item of food they bought at a shop — perhaps an alliterating item (e.g. 'My name is Michael and I bought milk'). All of the items could then be combined as the only food left for a group abandoned on an island. (Don't reveal this before the game!)

4 Students add a rhythmic clicking of the fingers: two clicks before they call their names. This can be changed to clicking and calling the name of another person in the circle, who will then call someone else's (e.g. click-click 'Hannah'; click-click 'Michael'). The ensuing drama could use the tension this game creates to explore how people work under pressure.

5 If the students already know each other's names, they can choose a pseudonym (e.g. Gargantua) or a name they wish their parents had given them (e.g. Elvis). If the drama is to be based on a novel, they could choose the names of characters or role functions (e.g. 'I'm Erica' or 'I'm the grocer'), and this could become the basis for some improvisational work on incidents from the novel.

Movement games can make students comfortable with the spatial context for the drama and help mix the group. Here are a couple of examples.

The sun shines on. Students sit on chairs in a circle while you stand in the centre. You identify some visible feature or object or quality that some of the students share (e.g. 'The sun shines on all people with curly hair/wearing a watch/in sneakers'). Those who fit the category must stand and change chairs with someone else. This can be done slowly until the game has been learned; then you join in, sitting on a chair, so that each round ends with a student in the centre to choose the next category. You can allow yourself to be 'caught' if you want to re-establish control of the category naming: equally you can stop the game when you see that students are sitting separate from their usual partners, or when the boys are mixed with the girls. You can vary things by speeding up the pace or allowing non-visible categories (e.g. 'all people who own pets/have brothers'). The ensuing drama could use pairs or triads of the newly mixed students, categorised as 'neighbours who dislike pets', etc.

Tag. One student is 'It' and hunts the others, who can be saved only by grouping in the numbers you call out (e.g. threes). Once caught, students join the hunter in catching the others, leading into an 'us or them' drama.

A less physical but noisier tag involves students closing their eyes and listening for sounds (e.g. animal calls) that identify like characters for them to join. This could be the basis of a drama where different animal groups debate the use of a forest area.

Working with a partner or small group in a game can be the first step into a gradually deepening drama.

Mirrors. With partners sitting on the floor facing each other, B becomes the image of A in the mirror. A moves one or both hands, slowly and silently, allowing B to simultaneously duplicate the movements. Then you freeze the movement and B takes over the lead. When this game works the partners anticipate each other's actions, holding muscles slightly tense to correct any wrong guesses about their partner's next move.

You can of course specify the action to be mirrored — an inexperienced cook preparing a meal, a woman dressing for dinner, a clown putting on makeup — and the mirroring can then become the first step in a drama about a dinner party or a circus. The game can also be used at the mid-point of a lesson to help students further into the drama, or at the end to help them de-role.

Mirroring talk. Two lines, A's and B's, face each other. The A's describe their morning slowly and clearly to the B's, who attempt to speak along with them by anticipating their words and watching their mouths as they speak. At intervals you freeze the talk and partners change; the A's continue their original stories with their new partners (who will accumulate a range of fractured stories). Any combination of the stories can become the basis of a drama.

Master/servant. A and B take it in turns to issue and obey orders (e.g. 'Sit, fold your arms and hum'). You may need to emphasise that orders should not be humiliating to the partner. A variation is for one of the partners to be blindfolded and safely guided, by word or touch, around the room; then the following drama could explore the notion of status and the need for trust.

Storytelling with objects. A gives an object to B, who is blindfolded, and asks questions to lead B to a story (e.g. 'What does this feel like? What does it remind you of? What character does it suggest to you? What are they wearing?' and so on). Then the roles are reversed, B leading A with a different object. The two characters created can develop an improvised scene to begin a drama.

Improvising with objects. A and B share an object, which becomes something found at a sale. Each must attempt to argue (politely) why they need it. At the end of the game some of the discussions can be pooled to become the basis of a drama about the commercialisation of Christmas.

Students can develop lateral thinking with a game where objects passed around the circle are used in imaginative ways (e.g. a tambour becomes an earring or a mirror, a glue stick becomes a torch, etc.). Some of these objects could then be linked into a drama about a magical world where nothing is as it seems.

Games during or after a drama

Games are not only used as a way into drama. As shown in the examples below, they can be introduced during a drama for pausing and refocusing, or at the end to consolidate the experience.

Grandma's footsteps. Also known as 'Red light/green light', this can be adapted to serve as a pausing game. The rules are that one person — the watcher — stands at one end of the room, back turned. The group attempts to sneak up on the watcher, who suddenly turns; anyone caught moving is 'out'. In a drama about landing on an alien planet, the game might be introduced after several scenes (e.g. choosing the crew, near-mutiny, landing) as a way of slowing the action and focusing on the need for caution. The watcher serves as guard of the spaceship and the rest of the group become natives of the planet Jupiter. The number of guards can be increased if you want the Earthlings not to be overwhelmed.

Find the hands. Partners face each other and get to know each other's hands by touch. Then, blindfolded or keeping eyes closed, they join a larger group and explore hands until the partner is found.

This game can be placed at the end of a drama where differences have been resolved — perhaps different tribes at peace with each other or family members reconciled. It serves to cement the feeling of 'togetherness' and leads easily into de-roling and a discussion of the affective learning.

Conclusion

Drama games have many more uses than just 'warming-up' the class or marking the break between two periods. As long as you have a purpose for the whole lesson, games can form an important and challenging part of it, and they can be placed wherever they will best contribute to the desired outcome. Many games were invented to help people cope with actual events (remember *Ring-a-ring-a-roses* and the plague) and, used appropriately, they can help students to focus on particular issues.

3 MOVEMENT, MIME AND STILL IMAGE: BEGINNING IN DRAMA

Concentrating on body movement rather than other channels of meaning is often a useful way of beginning drama with primary age children. Enactment is, after all, at the heart of drama, and a major part of enactment is using the body to express other people's attitudes and ways of feeling and thinking. Observing and exploring the meanings generated by bodies moving in space can ease children into other modes of drama.

Movement, mime and still image all help to develop skills in observation and concentration, and they are also good methods of helping new arrivals in the country, or new speakers of English, to bridge cultural boundaries. Furthermore, working without words can be more manageable for young and inexperienced students — it's a more tangible way of expressing what they've observed about the world.

Although movement is instinctive and intuitive for all of us, living in a particular culture teaches us to use our bodies in particular ways. Working with bodily expression can lead to discussions which compare and deepen different understandings of why people act as they do. Before crossing the road in Australia, for example, we're taught to stand and look left, right and left again to check that there's no oncoming traffic. In a busy city in China, however, we'd have to step onto the road before any oncoming driver or cyclist would realise that we were serious about getting across. Then we'd probably have to freeze in the middle and pray for the traffic to go round us.

Relaxation exercises

Relaxation exercises can provide a useful beginning (and ending) for movement activities because they help students put aside other issues and focus on their bodies. They also break the nexus with sitting-at-table activities. Those of you who haven't used relaxation exercises before can be assured that the following procedures are 'tried and true' starting points. Further ideas are to be found in Steve Matthews' *Getting into the Act* (1988).

1 Ask students to find a space on the floor where they won't be disturbed by touching anyone else. Insist that there's to be no talking. Play some relaxing music and ask them to take deep breaths to the count of four, and then hold for four before exhaling. Gradually nominate each part of the body, beginning with toes and feet or head and shoulders and moving from one end to the other. Suggest that students consciously tense each body part in succession and then allow it to become heavy and relaxed.

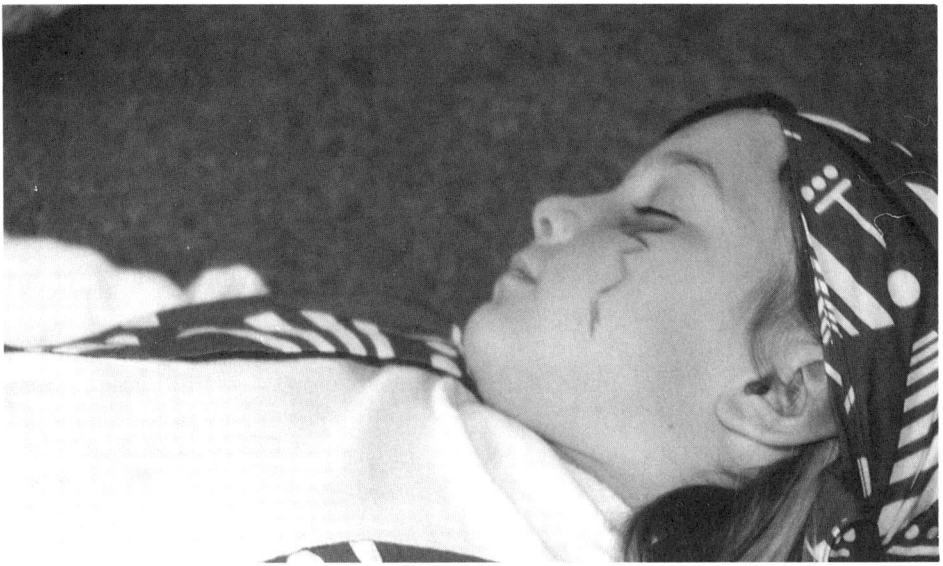

Relaxation exercises enable students to move away from 'today' and focus on their bodies, as well as the drama activities planned.

2 If there's not enough space for all the students to lie down, begin with stretching exercises. Again stipulate that students shouldn't touch each other. Suggest that they imagine they are stretching with all their might towards the ceiling to touch something that's just out of reach. Then nominate each body part in isolation (again moving from one end of the body to the other) and demonstrate the actions as you suggest them. For example: 'Your head's all floppy. Move it gently from side to side, then around in a circle — first one way, then the other. Now turn your head to the right, pretending that you're trying to hear your sister's conversation through the wall. Now do the same to the left.'

Movement

In order to understand how actions convey meanings, we need to understand how our bodies are located, both in the space immediately surrounding us and in the larger space shared by the group. Students can begin developing their awareness of space by exploring their own personal space. They can, for example, move around the room carrying their space as an imaginary capsule, taking care not to bump or intrude on anyone else's capsule. They can think about how closely they stand when talking with friends, and contrast this with the distance they keep when speaking to people they don't really know or with whom they feel less confident. In time they'll come to realise that different people require different amounts of space, and that an invasion of personal space can appear threatening.

Moving around the room making use of high, middle and lower levels can help students become aware of the infinite ways we use our bodies to communicate ideas, emotions or events. To highlight this, you may initially need to provide movement suggestions for the whole class. Students can think of themselves as a silk scarf fluttering to the ground, a piece of wallpaper slowly peeling from the wall, or a dob of margarine or butter simmering in a frying pan. They can be encouraged to use every level of their space, side to side as well as up and down. Mirror activities in pairs can help them explore all the space in front of them, just as choosing three different spots in the room and moving to each in turn can help them expand their use of available space.

Percussion instruments are useful for establishing rhythm and tempo. Tambourines and drums particularly produce a variety of sounds which can spark children's imaginations, as well as helping them to vary the pace at which they move. Tapes of a variety of music (e.g. Handel's *Water Music*, Vivaldi's *Four Seasons* and Grofé's *Grand Canyon Suite*) are handy to have to create a desired mood.

Still image

Defined by Byron and Griffin (1984, p. 25) as 'action arrested or frozen and therefore available for scrutiny and reflection', still image is an extremely valuable drama strategy to introduce early on. It involves students in using their bodies to create an image (sometimes called a frozen moment, depiction or tableau) that represents how a selected moment or incident might look. Just as photos are taken to record particular instants and occasions, or the pause button on the video is pressed to examine a significant frame for a bit longer, so still images allow attitudes and feelings to be captured at one point in time. Observing the images can lead to discussion and further reflection — even a second image — for, as Ericksson (1990, p. 13) remarked, 'Pictures may open up new understanding where words have forced us to think in grooves'.

One way of creating a still image is for students to become 'sculptors', using the bodies of other students as 'thinking clay' to shape their own interpretation of a significant moment. For example, a student might sculpt the final scene in *The Paper Bag Princess* (Robert Munsch), using three classmates to depict Ronald, Elizabeth and the exhausted dragon. He or she will need to find a way to demonstrate Ronald's disgust at Elizabeth's appearance and Elizabeth's contemptuous response. The students being sculpted take no part in the design process, though they may need to check that they are accurately representing the sculptor's intentions.

Still images can also be made by small groups shaping themselves into a represen-tation of a significant moment. Members can take turns to step out of the group and give directions, or one can act as 'director'. Groups can equally well choose a sequence of significant moments from a story to present as a series of freeze frames. However, it's important to discuss with

One student sculpts another to reflect his image of a pirate. The sculpted student must remain malleable to accurately represent the sculptor's intent.

them the reasons behind their choice of moments, for it is often through such discussions that learning becomes clear.

Working on still image in a small group helps students to translate thoughts, ideas or critical incidents into a tangible form which can then be discussed and, if necessary, remade. The focus is on group interpretation rather than on individual effort, and this development of collaborative enterprise is an essential concept to foster in drama work.

Once presented, still images can be 'unfrozen' and animated for a few moments of improvisation. Alternatively the teacher or another student may simply 'tap in' to each character's thought or feeling by lightly touching each one on the shoulder. If the characters are limited to one or two words in response, they have to focus on communicating through movement.

Still image can be also used to explore real issues that students are facing in the playground or classroom. They might be asked, for example, to present an image of a conflict situation they've recently experienced. Similar issues can be reflected in an appropriate fictional context. For example, Frances Oliverio chose the picture book *Willy and Hugh* (Anthony Browne) as a starting point for exploring issues of friendship with a Year 1 class. First she asked her students to use their bodies to show how Willy was feeling at the beginning of the story (i.e. rejected, alone) and contrast this with how he felt after making friends with Hugh (more self–confident, happier). In a subsequent lesson they sculpted each other to portray these feelings. Finally, before the ending of the text was shared, they were asked to create a freeze frame that might conclude the story.

The same approach can be taken in presenting and discussing images of issues in which students are not so directly involved, such as euthanasia, pollution, land rights or drug addiction. Their awareness of such critical issues will be heightened, along with an understanding that there are always a number of perspectives which need to be understood before judgements are made.

A drawing made by a Year 5 student after sculpting a significant moment early in The Cay *(Theodore Taylor) when Timothy and Phillip find themselves on a raft in the middle of nowhere.*

Mime

Loeschke (1982, p. 4) claims that mime was one of the earliest mediums of self-expression, used to give dramatic form to myths and other traditions. It was a feature of the earliest theatres in Japan, China and Greece, and it remains an important means of communicating to an audience. Although mime has had many definitions, it's best understood as the use of the body to explore or communicate an idea, concept, emotion or story. Usually it's performed wordlessly. Some purists insist on complete silence, eliminating any music or sound effects, but in the classroom it's sufficient for meaning to be concentrated mostly in chosen movements of the body.

Mime encourages students to use their memories and look closely at the physical world, to carefully observe others and become more aware of how they communicate non verbally with their own bodies. It gives opportunities for representing actions or emotions precisely and imaginatively, with the stress either on exploring or communicating them.

When you're preparing for mime activities, you may find it helpful to begin with the sort of isolation and relaxation exercises mentioned earlier, so that students can develop their awareness and control of different parts of their bodies. There are other activities, too, that may help them to change gear and focus on the coming drama — for example, they can be asked to:

- walk around the room, moving as they would move if they were feeling happy/angry/shy/proud, and so on
- convey an urgent message (e.g. *Quick, come over here!*) first with hands only, then with feet, and finally with whole bodies
- in pairs, give and receive a gift, conveying what it is through the giver's actions and gestures and the receiver's response
- mould an imaginary lump of clay into a recognisable object through mimed action around the class circle
- pass a nominated imaginary object (e.g. a hot plate, a wet rag, a handful of limp spaghetti) around the class circle.

A young or inexperienced class may find it easier to begin miming activities as a whole group. You can lead them by narrating a story while they mime actions, events or feelings as the story unfolds. A variation on this is what Peter Slade (1973, p. 30) has called 'the ideas game', in which students suggest three things for the teacher to link into a narrative. Usually one will involve movement and the use of space: for example, the students might offer 'hat', 'bicycle' and 'Christmas Day', which can be linked into a narrative about a family celebration. The story told should have some connection with the focus of the lesson. If you were looking at the concept of homelessness after war, for instance, you might begin your story like this:

> We are very cold and tired because we've been walking all day. We've been walking across fields covered in snow. The wind is bitter and blowing in our faces, and it's becoming very hard to keep going. But we know that if we stop we'll get even colder. We're so wet that our bodies are very heavy. Our legs feel as if they're made of lead . . .

Later, you might use percussion instruments to develop a tense moment, highlight a pause or represent the mood being conveyed.

With mime in the classroom, the emphasis is on detail and accuracy in depiction rather than on artistry and technique. Successful mime requires both actors and audience to suspend their disbelief and accept the illusion being created. When someone mimes lifting a large, heavy box, for example, the audience must feel that it's large and heavy because of the position of the body, the outstretched arms and the facial exertion. To mime eating a ripe mango means evoking the sensations of its taste, smell and slippery flesh purely through movement and gesture.

Mask and mime
Putting on a mask can be symbolic of stepping out of one's own self to take on another role, and so masks can be helpful in introducing children to mime, especially those who are reluctant to try it out. Simple masks can be made from paper plates or material and elastic, and even the ubiquitous red clown nose will serve as an initial form of mask. Neutral or universal masks are easy to make from plaster bandages and can represent countless characters. They illustrate particularly well how the body can be used to convey ideas and emotions which we usually rely on the face to portray.

Conclusion

Collaborative processes are highlighted when students begin using movement, mime and still image. If the experience is to be coherent and they are to feel its value, they have to work together, accepting each other's offers in mime and movement sequences or in depicting significant moments. Often these cooperative features of drama need to be explicitly discussed at the outset of a session and during the debriefing.

4 EXPLORING TEACHER IN ROLE AND MANTLE OF THE EXPERT

Teacher in role and mantle of the expert are two drama techniques which can really begin to change the dynamics of the classroom. They enable students to walk in someone else's shoes and at the same time confirm the importance of their own understandings and experiences. Yet though both strategies are useful right across the key learning areas, they remain underused in primary classrooms. So this chapter discusses first the rationale for using teacher in role, exploring ways of introducing it to students; then it explains the notion of mantle of the expert (which usually works best if teachers get into role with their students).

The rationale for using teacher in role

When Dorothy Heathcote first developed teacher in role in the 1960s, it was a controversial technique; the orthodoxy of the time held that child-centred, 'progressive' teaching should allow children's creativity to flower with little interference. Gavin Bolton (1984, p. 8), reflecting on his early contact with teacher in role, wrote:

> Like many others I resisted its usage at first, not because it was not effective, but because the idea of a teacher actually 'joining in' was more than my traditional teacher training and attitude to professionalism could stomach.

However, once Heathcote's technique was properly understood, it became clear that when the teacher took on a role and entered the drama world, she could unobtrusively ensure the child-centredness of the work, particularly if her role was of low status. Heathcote herself believed that it was the teacher's responsibility to 'be able to "forward" the work towards teaching ends without destroying the children's contribution' (Bolton 1984, p. 52).

Bolton went on to describe teaching in role as a 'unique pedagogical situation, where a teacher sees himself as teaching but the participant does not see himself as learning' (p. 157). He also cited Geoff Gillham, who had pointed out that there are usually two plays being developed in a drama class: the surface level (or 'play for the pupil'), where students focus on content, and the deeper, more symbolic level (or 'play for the teacher'), where the teacher's planning ensures that worthwhile outcomes are being pursued. Thus students in role as farmers may be enjoying an adventure in which they try various methods of settling a dispute with a bordering farm, but at a symbolic level, under the teacher's subtle guidance, they are examining the wastefulness of competition where opponents seek to win at any cost. However, the application of the drama metaphor to their own lives may not become clear until a period of reflection after the action.

'Child-centredness' has never meant restricting learning to what the child already knows, for unless the teacher promotes more than the status quo, there would seem little point in having the lesson. As Jonathan Nixon (1987, p. 21) has pointed out:

> The teacher must take the pupils beyond where they already are . . . and provide them with the information, concepts and skills necessary to adopt a critical attitude to what they already know. This is what is meant by the phrase 'informing the drama'.

However, with teacher in role, this 'informing' is often done indirectly: for instance, you can use your voice in such a way that you're giving information whilst apparently asking for it. You might say: 'I've heard that this time it won't be just the police we have to deal with; the government is sending troops down here to Eureka. I'm afraid! How can we defend ourselves? There aren't any walls to hide behind.'

In role, you can organise your students' learning from inside the drama world and use your adopted character for subtle pointing — or more forceful emphasis — when significant issues arise. For example, a decision taken by the students (in role as poor labourers) to accept money from an unknown patron will have consequences for the rest of the drama. You (in a low status role) can ensure that they become aware of this by interposing questions like, 'I'm not sure I understand why Carlos is offering us this money. Perhaps I'm too inexperienced. Can you explain it to me? Won't he want something in return?'

Teacher in role is particularly concerned with developing metacognition. Heathcote's comments on her work with children in role as pilgrims (in Robinson 1980, pp. 27–28) make this clear. She said that when intervening in role:

> I'm trying to show them the implications of what they are doing. I must create reflective participation. If I don't do that, I'm not in art of any kind and I'm not in learning. Also I want to show that in any situation there's a mesh of interests . . . You can best consider big themes by narrowing the situation right down.

The importance of careful planning

Although teacher in role (TIR) involves a high degree of spontaneity, it also requires meticulously planned scaffolding to encase the spontaneous work. Before beginning a TIR lesson, you need to plan how to engage the students' interest, how to elicit what they already know, how to challenge some of their preconceptions, how to extend their knowledge of content, and how to encourage them to reflect, metacognitively and affectively, on what they have experienced.

Steps in planning

1. The first step in planning is to decide on **content** and **outcomes**: what theme or topic will the class work with, and what might they be able to do, know or value as a result? Topics may be suggested by literature: for example, John Burningham's *Granpa* may be the starting point for an examination of memory, which is one of the themes of the book. Alternatively, a concern with newspaper reports on food contamination might suggest food processing practices as a topic.

    It's important to motivate students by choosing an attractive lure into the drama. Children can be lured by a photograph — perhaps one of Neil Armstrong walking on the moon — and a provocative question, such as: 'I wonder if everyday problems are more or less important when you're a long way from home?'

    Dorothy Heathcote and Gavin Bolton often began simply by asking, 'What would you like to do a play about?' If you follow their example, students' suggestions can be established in one lesson and, after some planning on your part, explored in role the next time. As you become more experienced, the planning can be done spontaneously and TIR adopted immediately. Furthermore, as older students become adept at what Bruner (1996, p. 161) calls 'going meta', the planning process can be opened up to them — the lesson plan itself becomes a fully shared experience, with students suggesting not only themes but episodes that might be explored too.

2. Having decided with the class on the theme or topic, you need to consider the deeper meaning or metaphor it might represent. By deliberately working in layers of meaning, you can begin to establish an aesthetic dimension to the work. Here it's worth noting what Stein (1971, p. 20) said about creativity: it depends on the student being able to tolerate ambiguity, on his capacity to 'exist in a state where he does not comprehend all that he sees or feels. Nevertheless he continues to seek resolution of the problem.'

3. Next you need to consider suitable roles for the class and yourself. Be careful to give the students roles which are interesting in themselves and not necessarily of lower status than your own. Because the work is whole class, it's usual to begin with a category of role (e.g. detectives, astronauts, farmers) which students can individualise as they wish. You can also suggest more specific roles for individuals by saying things like, 'Is the farmer who specialises in growing cabbages here?' Allowing students to choose their roles will strengthen their enactment because it allows for deeper engagement with the content.

    The role and status you adopt depend on what you see as the best way to facilitate the drama. A high status role (e.g. Minister for Agriculture) may not challenge the class sufficiently because it doesn't invite a response very different from their usual relationship with you. Equally, a low status role may be inappropriate with a new class, when the students don't know you or aren't sure how to relate to you outside your usual role. However, introducing a class to TIR with what Morgan and Saxton (1987) call a 'second-in-charge status' can be useful, because it means that in role you can't take final decisions but have to consult with your boss (who might be absent). Thus you can introduce delays, perhaps presenting yourself to the class as a character sympathetic to their aims. For example, in a role play where the students are vets wanting to inspect a farm for cow disease, you might be the farm manager who has to defer to the owner and asks for time to consult. None the less, when working with a K–6 class, it's most common for the teacher to adopt a very low status, 'the one who doesn't know', like the neophyte farm hand who's come for advice on feeding the pigs.

4   When first introducing TIR, you should be specific about what the students can expect. You might say, 'When I put on this hat [or scarf or spectacles], I'm not going to be me; I'm going to be someone different . . . Can you tell from what I say and do who I am?' Using the prop as a signal for coming in and out of role, you can interrupt the drama with narrative links to shift backwards and forwards in time. Sometimes, too, you'll see a need to come out of role to reflect on what's happening, or to get the class to decide, out of role and objectively weighing alternative possibilities, what to do in the next episode.

5   It's crucial to prepare your introductory in-role address to the class. What you say should induct them into the 'game' of TIR, letting them know (perhaps indirectly, depending on their experience) who you and they are, what the context is and why you are meeting. For example, you might open by saying:

> Thank you for coming to the upper deck. I wanted to find a space where the passengers won't hear us, and I think it's safe to say that they're all in the dining room now.

By now the students should have picked up that they are on some sort of ship (after all, it has a deck and passengers). It should also be clear that they aren't passengers themselves, even though they don't yet know exactly who they are. They might guess that they are the crew and that you are the captain, but before they can enter the drama world confidently, they need a few more clues:

> The captain has given me full authority to act for him. He doesn't want to alarm the passengers by leaving the dining room. You may have wondered why, when you signed on to crew for this mission, we made sure that you'd had at least some medical training. I'm afraid I have bad news: this spaceship shows evidence that the virus has come on board.

Now the students have a setting and a range of possible roles (they can build up or deny their medical expertise), and they know that you're only the second-in-command, not the one with ultimate control.

For TIR to work, all of the students have to be playing the same game — in other words, contributing to the focus set by the teacher. If they decide instead to 'pull focus' by having a heart attack, or to create an alternative tension (e.g. by inventing an imminent invasion by aliens), the drama may not work, and the rules of the game may need to be spelt out more clearly.

6 Because they are used to stories and the story genre, young children can become preoccupied with 'what happens next' rather than 'why this is so'. Heathcote has talked of the importance of 'releasing the ending' so that students can concentrate on what's happening now, and this may mean telling them how the drama's going to end — or even beginning at the end.

One of the strengths of TIR is that it helps students to pursue causes rather than the end result. For, as Byron (1986) pointed out, drama dwells in the present moment, allowing participants to choose their viewpoints and then use verbal and non-verbal sign systems to explore them.

Some features of TIR

TIR is a complex game of improvisation, involving 'offers' by both teacher and students. Part of the skill of teaching in role is being able to recognise and support a student offer which has real potential for deepening exploration of the theme, and correspondingly to deflect attention from irrelevant offerings. Thus, in the spaceship drama sketched above, a student might provoke a clearer definition of the impending disaster by saying, 'We had a sickness very like this one, but it wasn't fatal. Perhaps you haven't undertaken enough tests to identify the virus?' However, a student who said, 'I'm not a doctor; I'm one of the passengers', might have excluded himself from the drama proper and would need careful handling. It might be a good time for you to come out of role and clarify the implications of taking such a stance.

Bruce Burton (1991, p. 64) says of Heathcote:

> her use of drama directs the process of discovery towards a form of collective learning, involving a web of social relationships, rather than towards individual problem solving or cognitive and affective knowing.

It's largely through TIR that it becomes possible to hold a drama group together, at times testing its bonds and inviting individuals to think about why they are able to operate as a group.

TIR is especially useful for exploring common qualities amongst people who otherwise appear dissimilar. Heathcote has linked all such qualities in an area she calls 'universal', and plans to connect her students' experience with that of the characters in the drama by first discovering the 'brotherhood' to which all belong. For example, the medico-astronauts on the virus-infected spaceship and the students enacting the drama could both belong to the brotherhood of all people who wish to protect others from information that may hurt them. Of course, such thinking runs the risk of blurring important differences between individuals, and of calling things 'universal' when they are actually ways of thinking inculcated by particular ideologies. However, Heathcote's universals can be seen rather differently — as ambiguities or 'holding areas' for a range of interpretations (Simons 1997). From this viewpoint, the teacher in role explores these areas precisely because they can be interpreted differently by different people. Thus the astro-doctor who withholds information 'for the passengers' own good' might be challenged as an autocrat by a patient who is thereby prevented from healing himself, using his past experience of a similar illness in his family. Indeed, as the New London Group (1996, p. 72) has observed, in a multicultural world it may be more important to 'recruit, rather than attempt to ignore and erase, different *subjectivities* — interests, intentions, commitments and purposes — students bring to learning'.

In the course of using TIR, it may become necessary to find out what a character thinks or to have another perspective expressed, and then the technique can be blended with other devices (e.g. hot–seating) in order to deepen the drama. You might plan different episodes and structures, considering variations in pacing as well as perspective: sometimes the drama will need to be slowed in order to go more deeply into a topic; sometimes it'll be desirable to leap backwards or forwards in time to explore the causes or consequences of an action.

Mantle of the expert

The reverse of teacher in role is another technique Heathcote invented, called 'mantle of the expert'. Just as TIR was unusual in having a teacher work from a low status position, so mantle of the expert is unique in the way it elevates students to the position of 'the ones who know'.

A number of students are enroled as 'experts' in some enterprise (e.g. as historians or farm managers) and other participants respect their claim to expertise as they solve problems which they've been consulted about. Heathcote has continually refined the technique since the 1960s, and in its most elaborated form it involves the expert role being developed over a long period of time. The students are not merely told that they are experts — their confidence in their expertise is established through drama work in which their status is created and enacted. Mike Fleming (1994, p. 100) suggests that 'a group who will eventually advise on bullying may first establish their expertise as education experts by advising on the best height for school chairs, the appropriate range of colours for school crayons, or how to change a classroom to accommodate a blind pupil'.

The validity of statements by the 'expert' students isn't necessarily to be questioned: they are, after all, operating in a fictional world, and their status may collapse if they are challenged on minor mistakes. Thus, in a drama about an alligator, an expert zoologist who says that kangaroos come from Africa won't forfeit respect, since his claim doesn't affect the body of the drama. The true fact can be established later, if necessary, during a reflection period. In fact, it's often while students are in role that they're motivated to learn about a particular area or skill. Thus students in role as convicts transported to Australia might research details of a particular penal settlement in order to plan an escape, each working within this brief at his or her ability level. You could enter the drama as a newly arrived convict unaware of the escape plan, becoming again 'the one who doesn't know'.

Conclusion

Teacher in role and mantle of the expert are strategies which can be used to change the dynamics of classroom interaction beyond the actual drama lesson or unit. In both the teacher can be seen as a co-learner and students as actively owning their learning.

5 PROGRAMMING: USING LITERATURE AS A STARTING POINT

A drama teacher needs to be adaptable, to look for possibilities and explore the unknown. (Darvall 1992, p. 21)

This chapter focuses on programming teaching and learning in drama — both as one of the creative arts and as a strategy that can be used across the curriculum. While literature is the starting point for the examples included, any key learning area can be used as a beginning, and the approach can be either subject-based or integrated.

Drama is often thought of as a soft option and correspondingly undervalued. However, with six key learning areas in the primary school, the only way forward is to form as many meaningful linkages across disciplines as possible. Here the power and versatility of drama as a teaching and learning strategy is particularly valuable. Moreover, drama has unique possibilities for helping students to change concepts, attitudes or beliefs that are so much part of what Apple (1990) calls their 'saturated consciousness' that they have never questioned them or their implications. Drama makes it much easier to examine critically issues like gender, disadvantage or what it really means to be living in a country torn apart by war. At Harbord Primary School, for instance, Anna Dickinson used drama experiences based on Anthony Browne's *Piggybook* to focus the attention of her Year 3 class on gender equity and how it was manifested in the children's homes. She began by taking on the role of the depressed and overworked Mrs Piggott sharing her frustrations, and then invited the students to interview her in role.

The outcomes approach and drama

Before looking at any other examples, we should consider how outcomes-based planning affects the teaching of drama. The first point to make is that outcomes-based education causes a particular difficulty for programming in all the creative arts, not just drama. Bill Spady (1992), one of those who introduced the notion of outcomes-based education to Australia, has described three different kinds of outcome:

technical outcomes — essentially these are behavioural objectives turned around and written in terms of what you expect or hope students will have achieved by the end of a unit of work

transitional outcomes — these go beyond a technical approach to what can be achieved and observed over a longer time frame (e.g. what students will have achieved by the end of a particular year, or a particular series of units) transformational outcomes — these are the 'big picture' outcomes. For example, what do you really hope the students in your class will achieve by being in your class? What do you want them to take with them at the end of the year? Or, even bigger, at the end of Year 6 or Year 12? Spady suggests that we won't get very far in preparing people for the next century unless we start looking at the big picture in this way.

It's impossible to confine drama outcomes to the technical kind because we can't always observe what sort of learning has taken place at the end of a lesson, or even after a series of lessons. New understandings may be realised months or years later, and teachers won't necessarily be aware of achieving the particular transformational outcomes they had planned. When programming, therefore, they need to think about their long-term purposes as well as what they expect to happen as a result of a number of lessons.

The arts enable us to consider the way children learn in a way that other disciplines don't — for example, we can look much more at process than content when we think about using drama across the curriculum. Drama can effect change because it puts the learner at the centre of the learning process, and this is quite different from more traditional and technical approaches to teaching and learning. As Cecily O'Neill (1983, p. 30) observed:

> Every different art form will be likely to elicit a particular kind of experience. If it were possible to define and analyse that unique experience precisely, there would cease to be a need for the art form which produced it.

The drama process enables students to develop the sort of generic competencies (such as solving problems, taking risks and communicating effectively) that were outlined by the Finn and Mayer Committees in the early 1990s. Accordingly we needn't feel too concerned if drama teaching doesn't fit the parameters that have been set by more technical ways of teaching and learning.

Bringing about change

Jonathan Neelands (1990) suggests that the overall purpose in programming for drama is to bring about change. It might be change in a level of understanding, an attitude, an expectation, a social behaviour, a child's use of language, or in awareness of others and their particular needs. Some experience or trigger (which may come up in another key learning area) will prompt the teacher's decision to look at a particular theme or issue through the medium of drama. The students will be 'framed' in terms of some dramatic convention or form (e.g. still image, readers' theatre, teacher in role or mime). They may be framed as narrators, reporters/researchers, or perhaps as onlookers, and this will lead to the selection of a particular focus. Over time, after opportunities to work through the issues in dramatic form, teacher and students will reflect on particular things that have emerged.

Indeed, one of the most important things in teaching drama is to provide time at appropriate moments for debriefing — i.e. getting out of role and reflecting on the whole experience.

The overall plan must, of course, be broken down into reasonable expectations for the year, the term, the unit of work and, eventually, a specific lesson. Yet, as Darvall points out, each lesson must be seen as part of the whole, as indicated in the diagram below.

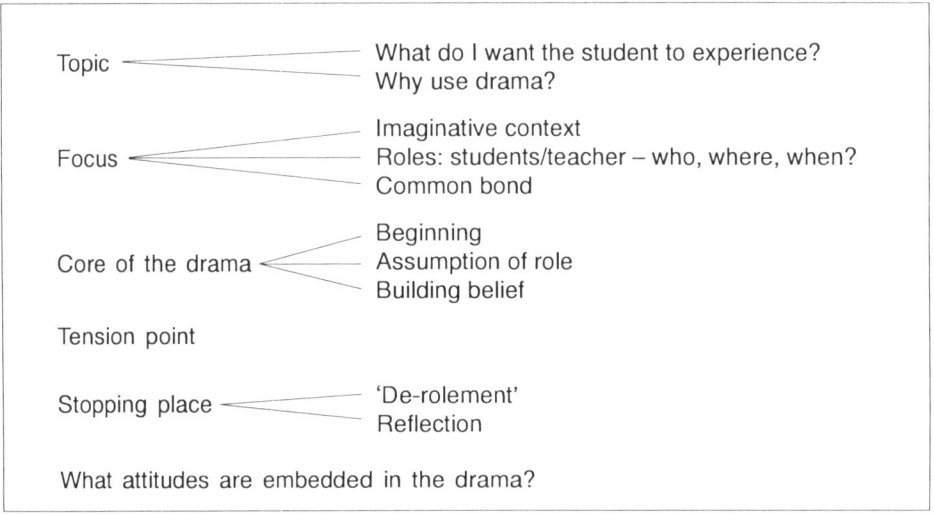

The considerations of drama planning (Darvall 1992, p. 31).

Programming drama in other key learning areas

While drama allows students to explore different perspectives, to step into different people's shoes, they don't have to accept final responsibility; the fictional framework affords them a degree of protection. Any issue can be studied with the aid of drama strategies — perhaps one that you're looking at in Human Society and Its Environment, or one in Science and Technology. For example, several years ago Cory Wilson, then a fourth-year B.Ed. Primary student, devised a unit on the threat posed to the Antarctic by mining (described in Wilson 1994). Initially she built up the students' field knowledge of the Antarctic and got them to explore what might happen if it were mined. Then she enroled one group of students as expert scientists, a second group as concerned environmentalists and a third as corporate executives who wanted the mining to go ahead for their own profit. The ensuing debate (in role) really helped the students to understand that such issues are never black or white, and that everybody brings to them their own interests and experiences.

Similarly, Jodie Stokes, who was working with a Year 4 class, challenged them to consider the advantages and disadvantages of war. Using *The Cay* (Theodore Taylor) as a starting point, she first helped her students to

Faye introduces Possum Magic *(Mem Fox & Julie Vivas) as a springboard for a range of drama activities she has planned for her Year 1/2 class.*

research the causes of the Second World War and then set up a debate on the topic 'War is a necessary evil'. The students used the viewpoints of Phillip's parents as a way into the issues and spent time depicting how each parent felt about Phillip's safety.

Another teacher, Lesley Sheperdson, used drama inventively for teaching Maths. Entering her Year 2 classroom as a sales rep from a well-known manufacturer of playground equipment, she briefed the students on redesigning a section of their playground using items from the catalogues she'd brought with her. The catalogues included illustrations, prices and dimensions of all the equipment. The students worked in small groups to a set budget, and they jointly constructed a questionnaire to ensure that other classes could contribute to the design. Allowing them to be the 'experts' in this way meant that they could develop new skills in a purposeful situation.

Programming drama using literature as a starting point

This section sets out a sample drama sequence, using devices already described in the previous chapters.

Text Jenny Wagner & Robert Roennfeldt, *The Werewolf Knight* (Random House).

Suitability   Years 3–4.   **Duration**   6–7 sessions.

Anticipated outcomes   Students will develop:

- knowledge about the characteristic ways in which different texts are patterned (e.g. fairy tales)

- the ability to use language effectively for different social purposes; skills of talking, listening, reading and writing
- the ability to ask questions about reading material rather than just accepting what is written.

(adapted from the NSW English K–6 syllabus document of 1994)

Focus It's important not to take people at face value. We need to unpack the stereotypes we hold in our heads.

Activity 1 Read the first page:

> Feolf was a knight and a good friend of the king, but at other times he was a werewolf. When the moon rose over the fir trees Sir Feolf slipped away to the forest, hid his clothes under a rock and turned into a wolf. All night long he ran in the forest, enjoying his dark and wolfish things; then when dawn came he turned into a man and went home. And no one was any the wiser.

Then explore the students' preconceived notions of werewolves. How much do they know about them? What do werewolves do? What do they look like? What else is known about them? Do the same with knights. Build up a database about werewolves and knights and compare them. Is there any conflict between the two notions?

Activity 2 Ask pairs of students to take turns sculpting each other as werewolves and then to think of words to describe how they expect a werewolf to be. The whole group can observe differences and similarities between each representation.

Activity 3 Ask students to recount stories, legends or whatever else they know about werewolves.

Activities 2 and 3 can be repeated to explore the concept of knights. The tension created by juxtaposing the two concepts can be discussed.

Read the next four pages of the text (down to '[Fioran] went to the court magician and asked him what she should do').

Activity 4 Use still image or sculpting to give students an opportunity to explore what's happened up to this point. How do they think Feolf felt about telling Fioran? They can divide into groups of three for one person to sculpt the other two as Feolf telling Fioran that he is a werewolf. One advantage of sculpting is that if you've got the whole class doing it, nobody is looking at anybody else. However, students who are less confident about how they think Feolf and Fioran were feeling can allow themselves to be sculpted by somebody else. Explain that if you're being sculpted, you really have to pretend that you're like plasticine or clay, so that the sculptor can place you in the position he or she thinks is most appropriate. Listen to the talk as the sculpting proceeds, and if you can't get around and hear every group, tape-record one while you're listening to another.

Programming

If it's appropriate, you can ask students presenting still images to give a sentence to describe how they are feeling at that point, or even just a word or a sound. (This is what's called 'tapping in'.) Before reading any further, send the students off again in groups of two to four and ask them to suggest what Princess Fioran should do.

Activity 5 Get students to explore what might happen now that a complication has been introduced. They can present orientation and complication fragments of the story as frozen moments and then improvise by adding action and words to explore what might happen next. You can 'pause' them by hitting an imaginary 'freeze' button and then hitting an 'action' button.

Activity 6 Hot-seat (i.e. question in role) Fioran, Feolf and the magician. If students aren't familiar with the hot-seating process, ask them to make a list of three important questions they'd like to ask.

The Werewolf Knight

The noble, gentle wolf was determined to kill the magician. However he was afraid because he hadn't killed anyone before. While the magician was walking through the forest he was whispering in his mind, "the princess is mine". So the anorexic wolf leapt over and jumped on the magician and attacked him even though he thought it was the wrong thing to do.

Princess Fioran was walking in the forest to fill her bucket with water. She saw Feolf on the magician. The magician was swearing at Feolf. Every time he swore Feolf scratched him. At the end of the day he ended up with over 1000 scratches.

A Year 4 student's prediction of how the story might develop.

Activity 7 Read on until the magician's comment, 'He has probably been eaten'. Ask students to walk around the room in role as guests at Fioran and Feolf's wedding. Who are they? Courtiers? Rich lords or ladies from a neighbouring kingdom? How did they travel to the wedding? What gifts did they decide on? When they've walked around the room and got used to their roles, ask them to stop and chat with a nearby guest about Feolf's non-appearance. What do *they* imagine has happened to the knight? You can then enter the drama as a guest who's been held up on the way and ask some of the other guests (now indignant) what on earth has happened. Later, after debriefing, the students can write down their version of the occasion.

Activity 8 In four groups (ladies-in-waiting, jesters, minstrels and cooks) students develop a sound or movement sequence to represent the gradual descent of silence and gloom on the castle as Fioran remains inconsolable.

Activity 9 Finish reading the story. Discuss with students the themes it raises. Are they satisfied with the resolution? Is it similar to the predictions they made?

This drama sequence can be enhanced if it forms part of a unit exploring fairy-tale narrative, or knights and legends, or the Middle Ages. There are many related activities in all the key learning areas which can be usefully integrated. In English, for example, students could develop a story map by expanding their initial sculptures or images. They might need to research some of the vocabulary in order to understand the richness of the language Jenny Wagner has used. In Studies in Society, they might research the period in which the story is set in order to assume their roles as minstrels, jester, etc. more authentically. Or they might choose to concentrate on a particular aspect of life, such as food, dress or transport. In Music, they might need to listen to recordings of the lute, harp or rebec, or medieval songs performed with an instrumental ensemble.

Conclusion

This chapter has used *The Werewolf Knight* to show how drama can be used to explore the understandings generated by a suggestive text. Remember, however, that success is not always achieved the first time these strategies are introduced. Failure is OK, and stopping and discussing this explicitly with your students can be quite productive. It is, after all, the learning process that's particularly enhanced by using drama strategies across the curriculum, because drama puts students right at the centre of their own learning.

6 PUPPETRY IN DRAMATIC CONTEXTS

A puppet is any object brought to life by a person. It is this life, transferred from the handler to the puppet and communicated to an audience, which creates the magic of puppetry. Young children often animate dolls, toys and other objects spontaneously; they become puppeteers without prompting from an early age. The puppet can be as simple as a box or a stick as long as it takes on its own character, separate from the person. Part of the never-ending appeal of puppets lies in the fact that the puppet is the focus of attention and so the puppeteer feels safe.

Puppets have been used throughout history in religious and cultural ceremonies, as well as to entertain and educate. In the classroom they can be used to break down barriers between key learning areas in a natural way. They will serve to:

- retell a story
- disarm the threat of taking on a difficult role
- prompt improvisation
- follow a scripted text
- resolve a conflict situation.

Puppetry is in some ways a microcosm of the drama process; it is both a performing and a visual art, and a teaching/learning tool across the curriculum. Students can practise oral and written storytelling, discuss the scripting and production of a puppet play, and extend their imagination as audience members. By making a wide range of puppets from 'junk' (sticks, pieces of cloth, egg cartons, etc.) they can develop their awareness of how a puppet can symbolise a particular character or concept. If they go beyond junk puppetry, they have to investigate more sophisticated methods of design and construction. At other times, depending on the context, they might have to research a particular era or historical event in more detail, or they might need to select appropriate music and sounds — especially if they're taking a play to performance. Working with puppets encourages people to express their feelings, and so it can provide a congenial emotional release for some students. At the same time students develop their abilities to cooperate and concentrate, and they gain experience in manipulating the puppet they've created.

Metaphor puppets and objects

A metaphor is a comparison of two things whereby one is said to *be* the other: for example, 'he is a lion among men'. In this sense puppets can be said to be feelings or character traits (e.g. happiness, love, fear), objects (e.g. trees, rocks), or symbols (e.g. coats of arms, flags), as well as humans or animals. Puppets are constructed from materials chosen because of their potential to represent some aspect of a character or thing, or its essence; thus a stern soldier might be suggested by a rigid torso made of sticks; a flighty character might have a body or hair of floating chiffon-like material. The materials that make up the puppet become a symbol for the chosen character, to the extent that the puppet is understood by the audience to be the character it represents. A puppet is therefore something like a three-dimensional metaphor.

As a metaphor, the Educational Drama Association (1981, p. 1) observed:

> the puppet is both an essence and an emphasis . . . it is more than its live counterpart — simpler, sadder, more wicked, more supple. At the same time, it may be less complex than the character it represents. A mere suggestion has caused the puppet to be filled with life and exert a universal appeal.

Thus it's important for students to invest each of their puppets with a name and with particular ways of speaking and moving that are the essence of the chosen character. Finding the correct tone and pitch for a puppet's speech and determining how it relates to other puppets is part of filling out the comparison.

Types of puppets useful in the classroom

Puppetry gives people scope to choose the kind of puppet best suited to whatever concept or theme is to be dramatised. Many types of puppets lend themselves to classroom use, and they are briefly described below.

Finger puppets   Often the most appropriate with young children, finger puppets can be knitted or made from toy felt sewn or glued together. Alternatively, they can be drawn or duplicated on stiff coloured paper with a 'ground level' strip to form a ring around the finger. Distractions during storytelling can be minimised if each child manipulates his or her finger puppet or set of finger characters while the teacher or another student reads or tells the story.

Paper plate puppets   To simplify the logistics of minor dramatic productions, characters can be made out of paper plates attached to a ruler or a piece of firm cardboard to make manipulation easier. The script or outline for the performance can be stuck on the back.

Paper plate puppets

Shadow puppets   Shadows formed by hands or cut-out figures can easily be projected onto a wall or screen. The easiest way to begin is with 'Fuzzy Felt' or paper figures, perhaps with cellophane-filled cutouts to add colour. To avoid hand shadows, students can manipulate the figures with knitting needles or sticks fixed to the back. Simple scenery drawn on acetate sheets — perhaps coloured — can be placed on an overhead projector.

Hand or glove puppets   These are the most versatile and popular puppets of all. They are probably the best to use for scripted plays, when stages, scenery, etc. can be used as well. While heads can be made from a variety of materials (e.g. paper mâché or fabric), the polystyrene ball method is recommended for uniformity of product and speed of construction (see overleaf). Students can each make a puppet at the beginning of the year to provide a class or school set. This will encourage the frequent use of puppets in improvisation, as well as in more formal activities across all key learning areas.

Ventriloquial puppets   Ventriloquial puppets make frequent appearances on TV programs like 'Sesame Street', and they are often used as learning tools with children in K–2 classrooms. Their soft bodies and contours and lack of 'personal' dominance make them attractive to children and adults alike.

Marionettes and rod puppets   These are generally too complicated for primary students to make easily, and in any case they don't lend themselves to classroom use.

Masks   An actor defines his character partly by dress. A mask does the same thing more economically, but brings the actor closer to the puppet by denying or restricting the use of one of his most expressive features — his face. Full-face masks can of course be decorated more elaborately than half-face or eye masks. Masks can also be reduced even further — to labels stuck on foreheads, paper bird beaks taped to noses or red clown noses attached with elastic — and they can be labelled as objects, concepts, numerals, names, etc.

It's beyond the scope of this chapter to examine puppet construction in any detail. However, many craft books abound with instructions on how to make a range of puppets, from junk puppets to more formal and longer-lasting ones. The most comprehensive guide is *Puppet Drama* by Robert and Jill French (1991), soon to be reissued by Scripture Union.

Beginning with puppets in the classroom

Puppets can be used to improvise, mime, dance, perform a scripted play, or even perform a circus. The suggestions for starting which follow assume that students have already made a puppet, either from junk materials or more carefully, over a period of time, as part of a Visual Arts or Technology and Design unit.

Movement and space   Divide students into pairs and ask them to imagine that A's hand is shy and B's hand is trying to make friends. What

Making a polystyrene ball puppet head

The following instructions can be used as a guide, but refer to Robert and Jill French's *Puppet Drama* for more detail.

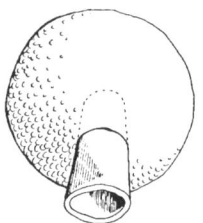

1. Make a hole in the ball for the neck, using an apple corer. Screw and/or glue in a piece of 25mm plastic or aluminium electrical conduit (available from hardware stores).

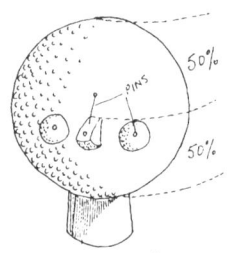

2. If desired, cut nose and/or cheek shapes from scrap polystyrene and pin in position.

3. Place a 20cm square of stretch fabric right side downwards with the maximum stretch from side to side.

4. Cover the backside of ball and neck with PVA glue and place the ball face downwards, with the nose in the centre of the fabric square. The direction of maximum stretch will thus be from ear to ear.

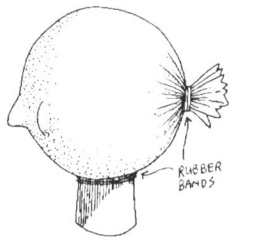

5. Pull the fabric tight so that no wrinkles mar the face of the puppet. Use rubber bands to gather up excess fabric at the back of the head and at the neck.

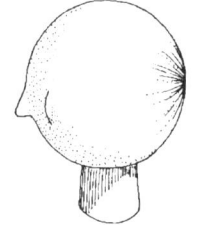

6. When the glue has dried, remove the rubber bands and trim off the excess fabric.

movements will they make in relation to each other? Then ask them to imagine that A's hand is an alien, to which B's hand is making a friendly approach. How will they interact?

Voice Ask students to introduce their puppet to the group, including a name and a few facts about the puppet, and using variations of pitch, accent, pace and tone appropriate to the character. For instance, a lion may speak at a low pitch, and if he's an aggressive lion, that will affect the tone of his voice.

Imagination Ask students to each have a one-sided conversation with their puppet, so that the audience hears them but only *sees* the puppet move as it 'talks' to them.

Improvisation Have students form groups of four with their puppets and ask them to decide:

where the puppets are
when the action occurs
who they are in relation to each other
why they are together.

To develop the scenario further, ask them to prepare and present an improvisation to the rest of the class. You might want to supply some guidelines (e.g. the focus should be on the concept of friendship, or the theme of the sea).

Staging a puppet play

Students need lots of opportunities for spontaneous improvisation with puppets before they're ready to stage a more formal performance. However, when they are ready, there are a number of principles to bear in mind.

Develop the play from students' improvisations.
Using a script from one of the numerous books available means that students won't 'own' the dialogue or action. When they're creating their own script, suggest that they keep the plot simple and include no more than three or four main characters.

Concentrate on action.
A lot of dialogue will distract performers from manipulating their puppets. Puppet movements need to be large and make use of the whole puppet stage. Encouraging students to practise larger-than-life movements in front of a mirror can be helpful.

Tape the script prior to performance.
It's hard for students to project their voices and simultaneously concentrate on puppet action. Taping the script in advance gets round this problem and allows them to think more critically about their characters' voices. Sound effects and music between scenes can also be included more easily.

Minimise stage directions and scene changes.
Impromptu stages can be simply constructed. A table with a cloth or blanket draped over it, a large cardboard box or a windowsill can all suffice. Backdrops can have cardboard cut-outs pinned to them. Simple, natural stage directions and minimal scene changes will enable students to concentrate on their puppet characters.

Props can be symbolic rather than realistic.
Although props needn't be realistic, they do need to be in scale with the puppets. Doll's house furniture can sometimes be adapted.

Lighting.
If possible, lighting should come from above the stage. Torches or angle lamps can be effective; even the light from a 35 mm slide projector may suffice. You can also try an overhead projector.

Conclusion

Puppetry can be enormously helpful for students who feel initially more comfortable if they can transfer the dramatic process to their puppet. It serves as a bridge to more direct dramatic presentations and helps to build the confidence and skills of students and teachers in non-threatening ways. It's also a very versatile teaching/planning strategy that can be used in all key learning areas.

7 PLAYBUILDING

The nature of playbuilding

Playbuilding is a sophisticated method of teaching which sets out to develop affective understanding of important issues across the curriculum. Its starting point is an agreement between teacher and students that together, through drama, they will pursue a sustained exploration of a theme or issue that they're interested in. The drama might begin with a wish to explore a general issue (e.g. pets), or it might be sparked by a much more specific question (e.g. 'Why was Alison Ashley such a goody-goody?') and broaden out. The students simultaneously create the drama and watch themselves and others participating in it. Facts can be seen in a new light as part of the emotional processing which occurs through dramatic experience.

All of the techniques described in earlier chapters (e.g. teacher in role, mantle of the expert, still image, improvisation) can be used in the playbuilding process. Those selected are adapted to the chosen theme, and sections of the drama are interlinked in such a way that the whole becomes more than the sum of its parts. However, there's no linear step-by-step model to follow, and so decisions about how the various techniques are put together are crucial to success.

Let's assume, for example, that your students want to playbuild on the broad topic of pets. In the process you might assist them to hot-seat pet-owners, sculpt scenes where some of these owners love (or hate) their animals, and improvise a scene at an RSPCA shelter. As the playbuilding proceeds, you might subtly focus their attention on a small detail mentioned during the hot-seating, redirect focus after the sculptings, or link the episodes by a narration which moves the story into the future. By these means you seek to deepen their understandings, or to build in layers of complexity that move the scenario away from stereotyped patterns. Sometimes you may want to involve your class directly in this sort of manoeuvre, laying the process bare with questions like, 'Do we want to see what happens to this cruel child ten years from now?' But of course that will depend on the maturity and experience of your students.

Playbuilding is a much longer process than students may be used to. It'll often continue over several sessions and may involve research. In some sessions students may need to recall what's already happened, and one option here is to begin each lesson by resuming 'the story so far', using drama techniques like round-the-circle stories or a series of still images.

The material which emerges from the playbuilding process needn't be presented to an outside audience; the 'play' may well remain incipient, with students electing to leave the process at the experiential level. For, just as professional actors need a rehearsal phase in which they experiment with the material to develop their own understanding of it, so classroom playbuilding is primarily aimed at developing the participants' understanding of the content. If the intention is to perform for others, then the focus of the work has to be shifted to communicating these understandings to an audience. Hot-seating, for example, is a powerful technique which may enable participants to penetrate a particular character's motives (it may also sharpen their awareness of questioning techniques). However, that doesn't mean that it's necessarily the best way of involving an outside audience — that may be done more effectively by converting the content of the interview into scripted dialogue.

Playbuilding, then, can either be a classroom process, where the participants create a 'play' for themselves, or part of a continuum leading to the blocking, scripting and performance of a play for an audience.

The background of playbuilding

Though the technique of playbuilding isn't new, it's been considerably developed over the last twenty years. The methodology owes much to the work of Dorothy Heathcote in the UK during the 1970s and 1980s, and her approach was introduced here by drama teachers who had either worked with her or enjoyed her video, 'Three Looms Waiting'. It's clear from this video that the children she worked with preferred to make their own plays rather than learning lines from a script.

Heathcote's famous 'What do you want to make a play about?' and 'I've been wondering whether you might be interested in finding out about . . . ' provided openings for her students to explore, from a fictional perspective, issues that were important in their own lives — what she called the *universals*. Her fundamental premise has been that cognitive and affective learning can't be separated; they are indivisible, and students learn best if they are engaged in the process of learning. As she told delegates to a conference in New Zealand:

> It's called drama because they didn't know what else to call it. It's really affective learning but it's built in cognition . . . (Heathcote 1988, p. 24)

Playbuilding began to emerge as a distinctive term in Australian syllabus documents during the 1980s. It seems to have been used initially in NSW: in 1984, for instance, the Sydney Metropolitan West Drama Curriculum Committee published an introductory booklet which included step-by-step descriptions of playbuilding episodes. In the original draft NSW K–6 Drama document of 1987, the term appeared (almost as a throwaway) to denote a process students might go through as they developed expertise with scripted plays. It has also figured in secondary syllabus documents (e.g. the 1993 NSW Higher School Certificate Drama syllabus). In 1994 the NSW

Writing Brief for the Creative Arts saw playbuilding as both a learning mode and a form of drama, and defined it as the 'shaping of unscripted plays'. Unfortunately, however, the new draft Creative Arts syllabus seems to suggest that playbuilding is merely a point on a continuum, implying that students must move from playbuilding to play writing, play reading and play performance. Yet this won't always be the case, especially in the primary classroom, where playbuilding may stop at improvisation.

Introducing and teaching playbuilding

Playbuilding uses all the elements of drama discussed in Chapter 1 (i.e. focus, tension, constraints and symbol). Any playbuilding process involves several essential steps, and these are described below.

Choosing the topic

While the topic must be concerned with specific people and places (the fiction), it also needs to extend beyond these specifics to a more broadly applicable meaning (the metaphor). Part of what the teacher will be doing in structuring the process is helping students to link their own lives by metaphor to the themes they're exploring. The playbuilding might appear to be about bushrangers, for example, but more importantly students could be exploring notions of responsibility, selfishness or self-discipline. Although the context may be historical, the metaphorical extension enables them to apply some aspects to their own lives.

Collecting ideas

Unless the teacher can help students to go beyond what they already know, the potential of the playbuilding process will be wasted. The process often involves researching the topic — finding such things as pictures, stories or newspaper articles that open it up. Some of these may be collected by the teacher and introduced at suitable moments; others will be gathered by the students as part of their exploration.

Starting the process

Playbuilding can start in different ways and a number of alternatives are discussed below.

Classroom discussion

A variation of Heathcote's *What do you want to do a play about?* may be the right kind of beginning for an experienced group of students. For instance, one Year 4 boy, faced with this question, came up with 'wardrobes'. His teacher was initially taken aback, but a little discussion soon revealed why wardrobes were so important to him. His parents had recently separated and he was angry at spending so much time between their two houses, packing and unpacking into different wardrobes. Subsequently a play was developed about relationships, divorce and its effect on children. The initial suggestion had provided a stimulus to open up some issues that were really important — and not just for that one student.

Establishing identities
Instead of exploring the thematic content first, students can begin the playbuilding process by establishing a role or identity. There are at least four ways to do this:

Mime allows students to represent a fictional identity. Examples which may require them to work cooperatively include:

- working in a mine
- making toys in a toy factory
- working as a group of clowns in a circus troupe.

Using what they already know or can imagine, students begin to externalise the characters of the playbuilding by miming what they do, and then go on to explore who they are and what they might encounter.

A **still image** can help to establish identities. Here's a useful one:

In groups of four decide which family member you would like to be, and then work out how each of you would stand for a family portrait.

Students can then think about how their family member would walk, talk and behave, and brief improvisations can build up the characters before they are asked to write a journal entry in role.

Movement offers another alternative. Ask students to move around the room in a particular way (through mud, using different levels, taking huge/tiny steps). Next ask them to imagine who is making these steps and to stop and talk (in role) to the person beside them. The accumulated roles might become a particular crowd (e.g. witnesses to an accident) that forms a springboard to playbuilding.

Sometimes an **object** can provide stimulus for a play — something like these:

- an 'old' map made by dyeing paper in tea and burning the edges may be the beginning of a play about what motivates and sustains explorers
- an old coin could be the focus of suggestions about why people go off in search of hidden treasure.

A particularly striking painting, text illustration or photograph can provide a similar stimulus.

Using music or song lyrics
A particular piece of music or the words of a popular song may evoke an image of a setting, event or character which becomes the context for playbuilding (e.g. the National Anthem for an event at the Olympics).

Exploring 'spaces' in a text
Oblique or implicit references in a text can be worth investigating. Students might speculate about the fate of the Wild Things after Max sails home (in Maurice Sendak's *Where the Wild Things Are*), or explore Princess Fioran's reaction when Feolf tells her that he is a werewolf (in Jenny Wagner's *The Werewolf Knight*). Each collage in Jeannie Baker's *Window* could be brought to life.

Recently a Year 2 class studying John Burningham's *Oi! Get Off Our Train* provided a whole list of endangered animals not mentioned in the text which could equally well have demanded a seat on the little boy's train. The children researched an animal they had chosen and were all hot-seated before creating their own train journey and, later, a readers' theatre script.

Beginning with a 'pretext'
Cecily O'Neill (1995) coined this term to refer to a fragment of information shared with students to seed a playbuilding experience — something like this:

> You've just landed on Jupiter and claimed it for all nations of the world. Suddenly you're confronted by the life force that lives there. This life force is very different from us . . .

A pretext can be specially written, or else an existing newspaper extract or a quotation from a book can be used. Pretexts need to be distanced and ambiguous and at the same time provide a metaphor for something important in the students' lives.

Scaffolding ideas
Whichever strategy is used to spark ideas, scaffolding them is vital to the development of the play. When a teacher scaffolds a drama, she shifts her students to a 'zone of proximal development', building a framework that enables them to move beyond the concepts they're expected to be familiar with. She uses prompts, cues or carefully constructed questions to break up problems in such a way that her students can deal effectively with each segment.

Scaffolding works if the teacher knows and understands her students and has a clear focus or direction for the learning experience. However, sometimes it is the students who contribute most to the learning. In a piece of playbuilding that Jennifer and Louise Quirk did with some students ranging in age from 5 to 14, the focus was survival/disaster and the play was based on a train smash. In one early episode the students decided that the cause of the crash could have been the incompetence of the signal operators, and this led to the question of how they'd been trained. The students established a railway school, and some were selected to tutor the others on how to become competent signal operators. When the tutors met separately to draw up plans for teaching signalling, Jennifer expected them to devise a flag system, but they set up the training on a computer-controlled system. The challenge had spurred them to apply their knowledge of the 1990s world to an old situation.

Edging into drama

When you're working on drama where emotions will be strongly engaged, it's important to use the fictional context as a protective device. For example, in dealing with a topic like 'How important is friendship in your life?' as part of the Personal Development curriculum, you might ask your class to draw sociograms of the friends they have and then think about other ways people can be friends. In Drama, however, you might explore the question by asking the class to think about two imaginary friends involved in an argument. Establishing a fictional context protects the students; it frees them to bring what they know about the world to this new situation without putting themselves too much on the line. They're still going to explore the notion of friendship, but the risk is reduced because they're working with fictional characters. Those who find it difficult to make friends might create or select a fictional character who shares this difficulty. Those who've developed some successful techniques for making friends will bring these qualities to the drama too.

Other ways of edging into drama include these:

Hot-seating can help ease students into the fictional world. Any character in a text or drama can be picked out for interview, and students can work in buzz groups to prepare questions to put to the character chosen.

Hot-seating this pirate enables the other students to find out more about his motives for starting a mutiny.

Rituals can be introduced to build belief in the fictional context — for instance:

> You will tell nobody of our decision to kill the inhabitants of Jupiter. Swear this solemn oath not to betray our secret!

This also exemplifies the imposition of a constraint (see pp. 7–8).

Teacher in role enables you to enter the drama with a different viewpoint from that expressed by the students. This will help you to deepen the drama or assess the students' commitment to what's being created. Think about your status when you choose your role:

> Excuse me, I'm very late. My carriage lost a wheel in a ditch . . . But tell me, why is the Queen crying?

> They told me that the palace cleaners might know what's happened to all the spinning wheels. I need mine to make a living.

Both these examples allow you to step out of your accustomed role as expert knower and bestow it on your students, who are then challenged to share their knowledge of a particular story or context.

Choosing and using **props** and **resources** is another way to ease students into fictional roles.

Providing appropriate resources

Props, music and masks can all contribute to deepening the drama. While you may have a basket of dress-up clothes and props and a collection of tapes, the students will be keen to bring in resources as well, especially as they become more involved in the drama. However, be careful not to allow resources to dominate what you're doing.

Reflection

It's essential to provide opportunities for reflecting on the process of playbuilding. Time to talk about the important issues or respond through journal writing, drawing or painting needs to built into each drama session. *Personal* reflections and the more *universal* applications are both significant (see Chapter 11).

Conclusion

Because of the time invested and the quality of engagement with the work, playbuilding makes it possible for deep learning to occur. In playbuilding students take time to construct an imaginary world, in which they invent characters, explore alternatives and solve problems. The fact that the teacher scaffolds their work to make it manageable means that they can develop confidence in their own creative abilities.

8 STORYTELLING: DEFINING WHO WE ARE

Storytelling is a form of drama which enables us to celebrate our own lives and experiences. This chapter draws attention to the importance of oral storytelling in helping us to define who we are within our particular cultural group, and provides suggestions for helping students to develop confidence in telling their own stories.

The importance of oral storytelling

Do you tell stories in your classroom? Do your students tell stories? Both the reading and the telling of stories are important and, as Colwell (1991) has pointed out, there's an enormous difference. A reader is always aware of the printed text, while a teller is able to speak directly and spontaneously and watch for listeners' responses.

> I'm beginning to realise the power of storytelling. It's a beginning to me because outside of reading books aloud to my class I had never really stopped to think about how often we all tell stories; out loud, in our heads, everywhere and all the time. These stories are simple anecdotes which are left undeveloped . . . (Newland 1990, p. 1)

Quite a number of teachers express a lack of confidence about storytelling as opposed to story reading, not realising how often we all tell stories and how important storytelling is to who we are. As a result storytelling isn't that common in classrooms, even though it provides a way of enabling students to celebrate their own lives and meanings. It's often an important precursor to the development of literacy too, and Carol Fox, well-known for her work in this area, has documented (1983; 1993) many of the oral narratives of young children, demonstrating how they learn to 'talk like a book'.

In what has become a seminal paper, Barbara Hardy said in 1975:

> Narrative like lyric or dance cannot be regarded simply as an aesthetic invention. Narrative must be seen as a primary act of mind transferred to art from life.

Since then there's been a lot of contention about whether or not narrative is a primary act of mind. However, the idea that narrative (or story) plays a pivotal role in the lives of children and adults alike has not been in dispute; after all, oral storying is significant in every culture — even highly literate ones like ours. Bernstein (1990, p. 78) wrote that 'the most dominant modality of human communication is not that of analysis, i.e. not the scientific, not the factual, but that of narrative'. Through stories we link up with the understandings of others; we begin to make sense to each other as we tell and listen to stories. There's strong evidence to suggest that children are capable of storying from a very early age, and many can provide some approximation of a story by the age of two. They use storying to sort out their own knowledge and ideas, and at the same time they are initiated into their particular culture by narrative.

Nevertheless many children come to school today without any developed knowledge of the traditional stories, fairy tales, myths and legends that we often assume to have been part of their childhood socialisation. So the loss is all the greater if the school doesn't give them access to a whole gamut of stories, not just from the western tradition but from a range of other traditions too. Making story a really important part of our curriculum is critical.

Some questions to think about

1. How do we use storytelling to make meaning?
2. How do we establish our personal or cultural identities through stories?
3. Do you agree that story is one of the few cultural universals? Why or why not?
4. How do metaphor and symbol relate to story?
5. What storytelling competencies can you identify?

Oral storytelling doesn't have an important place in the mandated curriculum documents of Australian schools. Even so, it's been claimed that some elements like newstime were introduced to promote the development of storytelling. Yet when Cusworth (1995) surveyed K–2 teachers asking why they programmed newstime daily, she found that only one of the 392 respondents identified oral storytelling as important in her classroom. Instead teachers claimed that newstime was programmed to facilitate the development of technical competencies like oracy skills, asking good questions (whatever they are), listening with listening manners (whatever they may be) and developing courtesy. Interestingly too, the small parent sample regarded newstime as the beginning of public speaking rather than as an opportunity to tell stories.

Research conducted by the genre movement in the 1980s suggested that children leaving primary school could write competent recounts but were less skilled at writing in factual genres. Subsequently we've realised the importance of giving children the skills to write in different genres, including factual ones like exposition, argument and information reports. However, in giving prominence to the writing of factual texts, we mustn't overlook the importance of fictional narrative. Equally there's a variety of oral genres that students need to be able to handle with confidence, and the structure of stories is one area that needs to be explored more carefully.

The structure of stories

Traditionally (going back to Aristotle's map of tragedy) we've been told that stories have a particular kind of shape, with a beginning, a middle and an end. In addition, many stories pattern their events around a central theme or figure. Other features commonly present in stories include:

- causality – to establish a plot
- temporality – to locate the story in time
- a particular context in which to locate the story.

Genre theorists (e.g. Martin & Rothery 1982) have suggested that narratives are texts which contain an orientation, a dilemma or complication, and a resolution. Yet oral narratives don't necessarily fit into such a linear framework (nor, come to that, do written ones), and the term 'resolution' is perhaps misleading. We must allow room for open-ended sorts of narrative which don't have a conventional resolution. After all, even though some of us may prefer the conventional happy ending, lots of stories do finish open-endedly, or with an unanswered question.

Nurturing a sense of story in our students

Children often come to school with a strong sense of story, though what kind of story they bring will depend on their cultural background. When Heath (1983) looked at three different sub-cultural groups of people living just a few miles from each other in the American Carolinas, she found that they had quite different ideas of what story was. The children from Trackton, who were black and working-class and belonged to a really vital tradition of oral storytelling, were skilled at telling stories because this had been part of their life from birth. When it came to creative writing at school, they were really good at telling the story. By contrast, the children from Roadville, who were white and working-class, had been discouraged from telling stories unless they'd actually happened — otherwise the story was a fabrication. They found creative writing very difficult, although they were much better at the technical decoding aspect of reading and writing because they'd been drilled with 'Sesame Street' and alphabet charts. It was the children from Main Town, the middle-class group, who'd been treated as meaning makers and had had access to storying and decoding from birth, who were much more successful at school because school required them to do both.

For those children not used to sharing stories, our challenge is to awaken their ability to do so. Both real and imagined storytelling have a place in primary classrooms. However, as teachers, we have to be careful that we

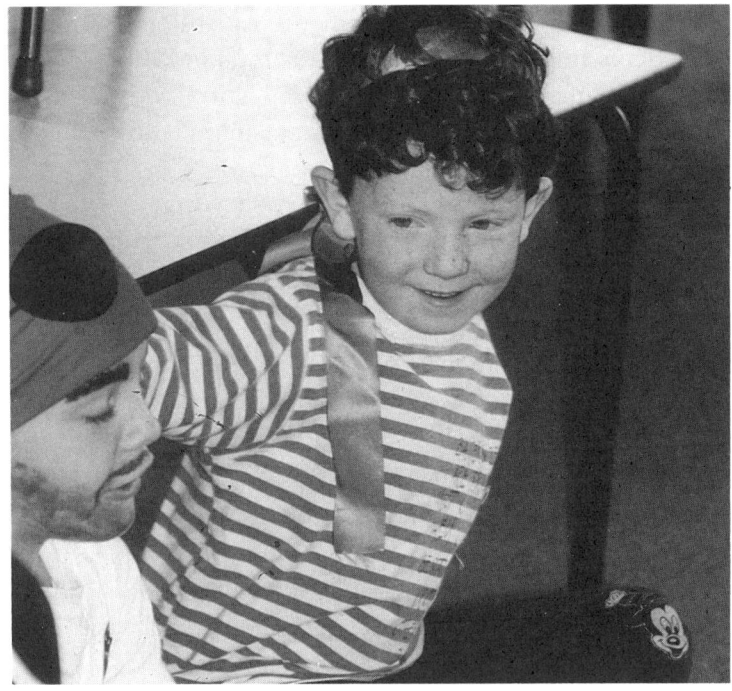

A student expectantly waits his turn to add a sentence to the story in a story circle.

value different sorts of stories. There's a lot of research, particularly from the United States, which suggests that teachers tend to be middle-class in orientation and that they favour stories which embody middle-class values. Thus they may implicitly put down or devalue stories from working-class students. There's also evidence to suggest that storytelling forms for different cultures are quite different. For example, the Aboriginal people of Australia tell stories which don't conform to the story structure described by genrists. We have to be very careful that we don't devalue different forms of storying, either explicitly or unconsciously.

Suggested storytelling starters

There are many ways you can help students to build up their concept of what story is, and a number of examples are described below.

Name games

Gather the class in a circle and begin by saying, 'My name is --- and I like ---'. Then you can build on this as much as you like. For example, you might ask students to start the particular thing they like with the same letter as their name, or to mime it so that everybody can try to guess what it is. (How much you add and how complicated the constraints you impose will of course depend on how well you know the group you're working with and what they're capable of.) The second time around, students might be asked to add some kind of description to the item (e.g. 'My name's Robyn and I like well-worn teddy bears'). Then, in pairs or small groups, they can share stories about these things and how they came to like well-worn teddy bears, etc.

Right at the beginning of the year, when you're getting to know a particular group of students, storytelling can be particularly valuable. For instance, there are some simple games that will help you learn the names of the children in your class (see p. 12 for these and other name games which can be extended into opportunities for storytelling).

Recounting an experience
Ask students in pairs to tell a story about something that went wrong for them once, or something that happened yesterday. You might like to model the art of storytelling first, pointing out that people will commonly relate the same incidents differently. Students might have a story about a favourite relative visiting, or a time when they were lost or frightened. Ask the listener to guess whether the story is true or fictitious, or a true story that's been embellished.

Beginning with a piece of music, an item of clothing or a sound
Some teachers like to use a piece of music (e.g. Dukas' *Sorcerer's Apprentice* or Tchaikovsky's *Nutcracker*) as a starting point for a storytelling session. Another way of beginning is to share a story about an item you're wearing and then invite continuations: 'I want you to choose something that you're wearing and tell the person next to you a story about it. Then swap over so the other person can tell a story.' Students have to decide whether the stories are true, fictitious or embellished.

Starting with a series of unrelated sounds can be extremely effective too. Ask students to suggest sources for the sounds and then string them together to create a story.

Three versions of a story
Three storytellers are chosen and seated at the front of the class. The first tells a story, the second retells the story but adds a different ending, while the third tells a different story using the same elements. The class is then divided into three groups to either mime or improvise the three stories, with the appropriate storyteller acting as narrator. If you need to divide your class into more than three groups, give one of them a different task, so that they have to vary the story again or use a flashback technique. It's often effective to ask one person in a group to act as narrator while the others mime what's happening (this is a particularly useful device with students beginning in drama, because you're giving someone a leadership role).

Using a role walk

Ask students to walk around the room in different ways — quickly, slowly, tiny steps, huge steps, etc. — and to imagine who might be walking that way. Just using movement may help them to think themselves into a particular character. Tap into these characters by freezing the movement, touching people on the shoulder and asking them to say where they imagine they're going, how they're dressed, etc. Put two characters together and ask them to improvise or mime a scene.

Retelling stories

Ask students to choose a story they'd like to retell and get them to read it as many times as they need in order to learn it. Drawing a story map and using this as a prompt can also be useful. Storytellings can be taped to enable students to listen to themselves critically. They may also like to practice in front of a mirror.

If you take the time to develop storytelling in your classroom, you'll find that students can translate their oral skills and begin to write stories which incorporate features like detail, motivation and characterisation. Instead of 'I want you to write a story about what you did in the holidays', how much better if you can say, 'I want you to walk around this room on your way to something or someone you visited in the holidays. I want you to walk the way you walked then, I want you to visualise what you were wearing that day, and I want you to think about how you were feeling on the way.' Give students time to make notes in point form about all these things before they write their stories.

Soon after embarking on a storytelling journey in his classroom, Tony Aylwin remarked (1990, p. 21):

> the greatest boost was the discovery that my audience didn't realise when I had missed something out. Once you know this you can concentrate on presentation, and in this it seems to me that hanging on to the shape of the story is all-important. It is this attention to shape, I suggest, that will be a major influence on children's understanding of story in all its forms, both oral and written.

Storytelling skills

- To keep a listener interested, the storyteller needs to use an expressive **voice** which effectively conveys the mood of the story. Ask students to say the same sentence several times, making it sound excited, angry, tired, etc.

- Students need to vary their **pace** as they tell a story, and they need to learn how to use pauses effectively. Ask them to read sentences and practice pausing in different places.

- The **pitch** of the storyteller's voice helps to convey the kind of emotion being expressed. For instance, how does the pitch of an angry parent differ from that of an excited child? Students need opportunities to learn how to vary the pitch of their voice to suit particular characters. Again, have them read over the same sentences while varying their pitch.

- The expressive use of **face**, **gesture** and **movement** can enhance a story, and making eye contact with as many listeners as possible is vital.
- Attention to how a story **starts** and **ends** is also important. Encourage students to visualise the scene they're introducing — perhaps by drawing a map, painting a picture or doing some simple research.

It's illuminating to observe other storytellers. Seek out opportunities to hear good stories — invite a storyteller to share stories with your class (many will have 'storytelling starters' to encourage children to share their own stories). You may also find that introducing rituals like a story chair or a special scarf or hat will help to set the right mood in the classroom.

A workshop for older students

1. Scatter a range of objects in the middle of the floor (e.g. a candlestick, a shell and a scarf).

2. Seat students in a circle around the objects and ask them to choose one.

3. Students who've all selected the same object form groups and explain how they relate to the object.

4. Groups construct a narrative to account for why someone has the object.

5. Students form new groups containing one member from each of the original groups (i.e. jigsaw grouping) and share the stories created in Step 4.

Relevant organisation
Australian Storytelling Guild
PO Box 76, Pendle Hill, NSW 2145
http://www.home.aone.net.au/stories/

9 READERS' THEATRE: FROM TEXT TO SCRIPT

Readers' theatre is a way of interpreting a story collaboratively. Syllabus documents often conceive of it as only about reading, or only about talking, but it actually brings together all four language modes in one dramatic form of storytelling. Its greatest educational value lies in the process of developing a script from a narrative, and so it's much better for teacher and students to create their own scripts rather than drawing on books of ready-made ones.

Readers can be arranged on the stage at different levels. They might wear a symbolic piece of costume or carry a prop that helps define who they are. They hold the script in their hands and focus their gaze at a mid-point above the heads of the audience. They concentrate on using voice, face and gesture to create the story in the minds of their listeners.

It's really quite difficult for students to understand what's meant by readers' theatre without having the opportunity to see it. If you're introducing it for the first time, it's a good idea to ask a small number of students to work with you beforehand so that they can model the concept to the whole class. Alternatively staff members can perform a script at an assembly.

Rationale for readers' theatre

There are a number of reasons why readers' theatre can claim a secure place in the classroom, and they are discussed below.

Development of small group skills

Setting up small groups of students to work on a readers' theatre script enables them to share and discuss what a particular text means to them. Subsequently they have to negotiate:

- how to reconcile differing interpretations to produce a script
- how the script should be read
- who will read what.

Working cooperatively to unpack the meaning(s) of a text can be one of the best ways to demonstrate that everyone brings their own prior experiences to anything they read.

Confidence in reading aloud

Readers' theatre helps students who aren't confident about oral reading to develop the assurance that they can read aloud. Many adults still have vivid, often unpleasant memories of oral reading around the class at primary school. Everybody in turn would read a sentence or, in later years, a paragraph — frequently from the school magazine. Some pupils would reckon up when it would be their turn to read and go through their bit to make sure that it didn't have any words that might trip them up. Everyone feared the embarrassment of mispronouncing a word they'd always read a particular way in their heads, only to discover that it was actually pronounced differently. Less confident readers would find the whole experience daunting enough to stumble over words or freeze up completely.

Oral reading is one of the hardest things students can be asked to do. Unfortunately young and inexperienced readers are often asked to read aloud from the very first year of schooling because, as teachers, we want to ascertain what strategies they're using inside their heads. Yet oral reading and silent reading are very different processes and require different skills. In oral reading, readers must process what's in their heads and look several words ahead of what they're enunciating. While it's sometimes necessary to ask students to read aloud for diagnostic reasons, it's imperative that we find ways to help them develop confidence about doing so. Readers' theatre can give them that confidence, and it helps them to practice their skills in a meaningful context.

Readers' theatre depends on reading a script to an audience. Even though the script may have become very familiar, the reader still has it there for reference. Readers' theatre is therefore extremely useful for children whose visual memory isn't well developed — children who, for example, wouldn't be able to learn a script by heart. It provides a bridge between choral reading and a fully rehearsed performance. It also gives students a scaffold for scriptwriting and editing.

Exploring the role of narrator

Readers' theatre helps to develop students' understanding of the role of the storyteller and the narrator (or multiple storytellers and multiple narrators). Where an author has employed multiple voices in relating a story (like Aidan Chambers in *The Present Takers* or Libby Gleeson in *Dodger*), scripting for oral reading foregrounds the use of different perspectives and opens up discussion of this technique.

Focus on voice

Movement, mime and still image (discussed in Chapter 3) allow us to focus on what we can communicate with our bodies using 'expressive silence'. By contrast, readers' theatre enables us to concentrate on the elements of voice which carry meaning — for example, accelerating and raising the pitch to suggest excitement. The voice is the most important instrument that anybody has, and the experience of readers' theatre helps students to focus on its potential.

Readers' theatre has been called 'theatre of the mind' or 'theatre of the imagination' because voice, reinforced by facial expression and simple gestures, can re-create a story in the mind of an audience more powerfully than can one person reading alone.

Enjoyment

Underpinning all of these reasons is the fact that reader's theatre is a tremendous amount of fun. We tend to learn most effectively if the learning experience is enjoyable — if we're actually having fun. In addition, as Patrick Verrior (1987) has said, readers' theatre helps students to develop a sense of audience. It makes a good beginning for learning performance and presentation skills, and it doesn't involve the teacher in time-consuming costuming and the choreography of movement on stage.

Adapting a literary text

Choose a text that you've been using for close study and that the students have enjoyed. It must have literary merit, lend itself to scripting and be a suitable length for the group of students involved. A picture book text often provides a useful starting point for those unfamiliar with the process. If you're using a chapter book, be careful to select an excerpt that lends itself to readers' theatre. A series of excerpts from a longer text, linked by narrative, also works well — as does narrative poetry.

The most appropriate texts will be those that centre on dialogue or telling something. Texts rich in dialogue are often effective as scripts because they come across more powerfully when they're read by a team of people than when one person is trying to command a range of voices. Some texts which consist of third person narration can be effective if they're divided among a number of storytellers. The opening of Ted Hughes' *The Iron Man*, for example, is very graphic when read by a number of storytellers because it turns on an echoing, question/answer device (even though it's not written as dialogue).

If you're going to adapt a copyright literary text for readers' theatre and take it through to performance before an invited audience, it's vital to seek permission from the publisher. Repetitions and phrases like 'and he said' or 'they said' may be omitted from the script, but you cannot rewrite the author's words. Any script must acknowledge the text and author at the beginning.

Initially you'll have to take the lead in producing scripts, but in time students will learn to do their own scripting (there's an example at the end of this chapter). Ensure that scripts include a number of characters and divide any narrative passages between several storytellers. If one reader has three paragraphs without a break, the whole point of multiple storytelling will be lost, and the other readers and audience may all lose interest.

Students begin to think about how they should read the part they've been allocated.

Starting with readers' theatre

Once your script is available in multiple copies, have students read it in pairs around the whole class. Talk explicitly about using the voice to emphasise important elements in the story. Then divide the class into small groups and either allocate parts within each group or allow group members to decide on parts among themselves. Initially ask groups to read around together and talk and think about how the script should be treated — how it might be read to convey different meanings.

Students can highlight their character's part in their scripts, which can be glued into manilla folders with the character drawn on the front. They can also think about a symbolic piece of costuming or a prop that will distinguish them from the other readers: for example, the three Billy Goats Gruff could have different sized folders. Students then practise their reading on a number of occasions, perhaps underlining words that need special emphasis. Characters reading the same part in different groups can discuss the way they interpret various lines.

Students can be encouraged to think about how they might arrange themselves on a stage in front of an audience. They might also consider whether percussion instruments or body percussion might be used to add emphasis at particular points, or whether other musical sounds might be more appropriate. For instance, Libby Gleeson's *The Princess and the Perfect Dish* is enhanced by the sounding of a melody each time the princess tastes the delicious fruit; Steven Kellogg's *Chicken Little* benefits from sound effects indicating that an acorn has fallen from the sky or the helicopter has come crashing down on the fox. Students can note any music or sound effects in their scripts.

You won't necessarily wish to take the reading of a readers' theatre script to full performance. Nevertheless there will be times when students who've had a really wonderful time with a script want to perform it. Such performances can be a fitting culmination for them — and for the rest of the class, or the class next door, or a whole school assembly. If it's decided to go this way, the readers will need some extra rehearsal time.

Children scripting

Once students have absorbed the process from your modelling, they can be given opportunities to script for themselves (though they won't become entirely competent overnight). With older students, you might find that a novel you've chosen for close study contains a passage that lends itself to multiple reading. For example, Libby Gleeson's *Eleanor Elizabeth* opens with the children in the car going to their new house. Eleanor is thinking about having left Brunswick Heads for a dry and dusty country town, how hot it's going to be and how she's going to miss her friends. At the same time she and her brother are playing *I Spy*. This part of the text really lends itself to being read by a number of voices. However, it's also a passage that students may need help with. There's an ongoing inner voice or stream of consciousness interwoven with lots of dialogue, and less experienced readers may need to be shown what's happening, who's speaking when, and so on. It might be a good idea to begin by scripting a little bit yourself, using the OHP or butchers' paper, and then give students the chance to develop a script themselves.

The Shrinking of Treehorn (Florence Heide) is a book particularly suited to readers moving from being heavily supported by pictures to working with chapter books. At the beginning of the story Treehorn starts to get smaller and smaller, but his mother doesn't notice or even hear his concerns — she's too busy thinking about why her cake didn't rise or spring-cleaning the house. When she finally does notice, she blames her son. There are all sorts of delightful snatches of conversation through the book: for example, when Treehorn gets on the bus and the driver says he must be his (Treehorn's) brother because he looks exactly the same but smaller; when he gets into trouble at school because he can't reach the bubbler, and when the principal interviews him for this misdemeanour. Small groups can script four or five excerpts, and these can then be linked by a narrative summarising what's happened between each one.

Writing scripts for readers' theatre makes students think about the role of the narrator (or narrators) in a text; about the presence of multiple voices; about the differences between spoken and written language, and about the power of their own voices to make meaning. Ideally they should try adapting some of their own narrative writing.

It can also be rewarding to combine readers' theatre with other drama strategies. For instance, one group of students can read the script while another mimes the action or uses a series of still images to represent critical moments in the story.

An excerpt from a student script

THE PAPER BAG PRINCESS
by Robert Munsch and Michael Martchenko
Adapted by 5B, Campsie Primary School

STORYTELLER 1:	*Elizabeth was a beautiful princess.*
STORYTELLER 2:	*She lived in a castle and had expensive clothes.*
STORYTELLER 3:	*She was going to marry a prince named Roland.*
STORYTELLER 4:	*Unfortunately a dragon smashed her castle, burnt all her clothes with his fiery breath and carried off Prince Roland.*
STORYTELLER 1:	*Elizabeth decided to chase the dragon and get Ronald back. She looked everywhere for something to wear but the only thing she could find that was not burnt was a paper bag.*
STORYTELLER 2:	*So she put on the paper bag and followed the dragon.*
STORYTELLER 3:	*He was easy to follow because he left a trail of burnt forests and horses' bones.*
STORYTELLER 4:	*Finally Elizabeth came to a cave with a large door that had a huge knocker on it.*
STORYTELLER 1:	*She took hold of the knocker and banged on the door.*
STORYTELLER 2:	*The dragon stuck his nose out of the door and said:*
DRAGON:	*Well, a princess! I love to eat princesses but I have already eaten a whole castle today. I am a very busy dragon. Come back tomorrow.*
STORYTELLER 3:	*He slammed the door so fast that Elizabeth almost got her nose caught.*

10 TAKING SHAPE: AESTHETICS AND DRAMA FORM

Drama is a method of teaching and learning, but it's also an art form, one of the ways in which we come to know the world. Each art form (e.g. drama, dance, visual art, music, literature) evolves within particular cultures and social systems and can either reinforce or contest the values of those systems. Sometimes the artist sets out to challenge the way things are (as Anthony Browne does in his portrayal of humans in *Zoo*); sometimes he or she celebrates the way things could be (as Nadia Wheatley does in her depiction of social harmony at the end of *Dancing in the Anzac Deli*). Working in the arts in primary school means working with feelings and beliefs, and conveying meanings through a variety of forms.

A Statement on the Arts for Australian Schools (1994) points out that students can be art makers, performers, audience members, critics or art theorists. So far in this book we've focused on students as makers and performers. But it's also important for them to learn to refine their skills as audience members, whether they're watching the work of classmates, enjoying performances at assemblies, or critically evaluating the presentation of plays by professional actors.

Making and watching

There's no need for a major division between students' activities as makers and audience members; the audience function can be developed in ordinary classroom improvisations. Cecily O'Neill (1995) has pointed out that even while students are actively engaged in a drama, they also have *percipient* roles: that is, while each appears to be fully committed to enacting a role in a fictional world, they are also watching, aware of themselves and their peers pretending. This may involve balancing contradictory emotions, or what Vygotsky (1976, p. 549) called 'dual affect' — 'the child weeps in play as a patient, but revels as a player'. Gavin Bolton (1987) has used the term *metaxis* for this ability to be in two worlds at once.

Role within role

There are several ways in which you can strengthen the audience function while students are creating improvised drama. One is by using the technique of **role within role**, where a character or event is not what it seems. O'Neill has remarked out that many fairy stories have characters pretending to be someone else (e.g. the wolves in *Red Riding Hood* and *The Three Little Pigs*).

Science fiction and detective stories also use role within role (e.g. Clark Kent really being Superman, or the butler being the murderer). Asking students to enact a role which is itself a role, like a witch pretending to be a good fairy, increases the 'watching' element. Reflection afterwards can consider how they've tried to suggest the ambivalence of the character.

Protection into role

Another technique which, as a by-product, sharpens audience awareness is **protection into role** (discussed on p. 2). Although its main purpose is to establish a healthy distance between the student and a risky enactment, it also strengthens the percipient function. For example, you might ask students to spend time drawing and describing a new settlement in space, using the fiction to ease them past emotional blocks that reality might impose, and then look at how the settlers might deal with aliens. During reflection after the enactment you could help them to see parallels with racism in the real world by deconstructing the metaphor. Realising further layers of meaning some time later is a frequent experience with theatre. As David Best (1985, p. 184) observed:

> The peculiar force of learning from a work of art consists in an emotional experience which casts a new light on a situation, revealing what the analogous situation amounts to.

It is becoming conscious of *form* that makes for aesthetic learning.

From making to aesthetic understanding

Children take on the more sophisticated functions of critic and aesthetic theorists as they become more knowledgeable and articulate about the form in which they work. Gavin Bolton (1984, p. 162) has argued that drama becomes aesthetic learning when children, absorbed at first by drama content, 'feel in their bones that somehow the incident is heightened, sharpened, condensed, etc. . . . they can learn it is form that makes the simple action significant'. He suggests that the process is for children to first experience a form where the elements of drama have been consciously used to create dramatic art, and then to be gradually made aware of how that form was created. In other words, they move from experience to understanding. Peter Abbs (1987, p. 53) says that in aesthetic activity we 'half-apprehend and half-create a world of understanding, of heightened perception, of heightened meaning'. However, as his use of the term 'apprehend' suggests, it's not always possible to put that meaning into words, and sometimes the experience may not be assimilated at the time of reception. 'Making aware' might mean helping students to express the effect of their learning in other ways — by drawing, for instance. Alternatively working slowly with sculpture and discussing it during or after the process can help students to weigh up the impact of different forms.

Creating a performance for others: acting and directing

Often teachers are asked to prepare and present a dramatic item at a school assembly or an end-of-year celebration, and the focus of their work shifts from exploratory drama to ways of communicating with an audience. Then, as Bolton says (in Hargreaves 1990, p. 129), 'the actors have to prepare themselves in techniques militating against spontaneity in favour of *repeatability*'. Sometimes the material has emerged from the students' own improvised drama; sometimes it's an adaptation of a book; sometimes they act in a play.

When students are working towards a performance, they have to anticipate the probable response of the people watching. A directorial role, an outside eye, becomes vital — someone to step outside the evolving performance and see it as the audience will see it, adjusting movement, spacing, gestures and so on until each communicates the desired effect. Preparing for performance often means using trial and error to refine what was at first spontaneously created; it means rehearsing until the students achieve a finished performance which they can repeat. If the students are inexperienced, the director's task is best left to the teacher to begin with, but it can be shared and gradually handed over. Even Kindergarten students can be asked, 'How do we want the audience to feel?' and 'I wonder what would make them feel that way?'

One advantage of developing a play from the students' own improvisations is that it engenders proud feelings of ownership. In addition, links between their experience and the fiction are assured, and the problem of having a few stars and lots of 'spear-carriers' or 'autumn leaves' is avoided. Refining an improvised play for a known audience makes it easy to incorporate local references — in-jokes, recognisable settings, and characters who appeal because they 'fit' the students enacting them. You can create leading roles for a gymnast or a yodeller (depending on who's in the class!). Play-building techniques (described in Chapter 7) can be put to good use here.

Watching others perform: the spectator function

Any successful performance requires the collaboration of the audience, and it could be argued that meaning ultimately resides in the interaction between the spectators and the makers of a performance. Theatre in education (TIE) is a form of professional theatre specially designed for children; performed by adults, it is usually presented in the audience's school environment. TIE first emerged in England during the 1960s, and the actor-teachers of the Belgrade Theatre in Coventry were the first to use the term. They drew on many of the same principles as Dorothy Heathcote, actively involving their audience by asking for suggestions on how to solve dilemmas and absorbing the answers into the flow of the play. TIE set out to teach about theatre as well as teaching particular content.

In Australia TIE teams like Toe Truck, Magpie, Salamanca, Freewheels and Zeal have made it their mission to bring good theatre to schools, and part of their practice has been to work with students after a performance, assisting in deconstruction of the play. Inviting such companies to your school is a good way to induct students into the experience of theatre, and TIE plays and actors both teach them how to be a good audience.

Recently writers who have worked in TIE have begun to publish scripts of their plays (e.g. David Holman's *No Worries* and *Small Poppies*). As these were devised for adult actors, they're probably too difficult for children to perform complete, though selected scenes are feasible. Other playwrights have adapted successful children's novels as plays: for instance, Richard Tulloch has dramatised *Hating Alison Ashley* and *Space Demons*, and there are scripts of *Boss of the Pool* (by Mary Morris) and *Puppy Love* (by Bruce Keller).

The experience of watching any theatrical performance is enhanced by discussion afterwards. Students need to talk about how they felt while they were watching and how they feel now. Given the opportunity to constructively discuss the way a performance was staged (and why), and how certain characters were portrayed, they will come to understand better the role of the audience in drama.

Working with a script

It's important to realise that reading a play script is one of the most difficult reading tasks, because readers are trying to do two things simultaneously. On the one hand they have to read 'aesthetically', empathising with the characters and events (which mainly involves the dialogue). On the other hand they have to read for practical information about how the play might be staged.

Scripts are really aimed at directors, designers and actors, whose collaboration is required to realise the full meaning of the text. Students reading a script need to read for understanding of the action, of course, but they also need to read for information about how to bring a performance before an audience — i.e. stage directions, other cues (such as pauses) and details of the set, lighting and costumes. Readers' theatre scripting (discussed in Chapter 9) provides a useful introduction to the nature of script reading.

The following strategies for working with a script can be modified to suit your class.

- Choose **drama games** which set the mood for interpreting the play. You can then adapt this technique to help students explore the subtext; for instance, a game about being the 'odd one out' (like *Pig in the middle*) might be useful for a play about Alison Ashley.
- Before reading, set up parallel **improvisations** (i.e. scenes which will evoke the same emotions).
- Prepare a **reading** of the script using the strategies described on p. 60.

Aesthetics and drama form

- **Hot-seat** a character to build up the background for a scene (e.g. Alison's mother).
- Set up **still images** to extract the main point of each scene.
- Have the class **sculpt** the characters at a particular moment. They can then talk through what's happening.
- Isolate **key sentences** or **phrases** (e.g. 'Erica Yurken, where do you think you're going?') and prepare improvisations which start or end with them.
- Have the class work in **small groups** as:
  a) director
  b) actor
  c) designer.
- **Drawing** — block each scene, showing where, how and why the characters will move.

11 EVALUATION AND ASSESSMENT

Evaluation and assessment issues are problematic in drama, particularly in light of the current debate on outcomes-based education. This approach often requires the teacher to observe changes in student behaviour, actions or attitudes at the end of a particular lesson or unit of work. Yet if we restrict the meaning of evaluation to immediately observable change in this way, we fail to measure the most important contribution that drama can make to learning. Drama can bring about shifts in perspective and develop the imagination; it can sow seeds for the making of meaning which won't necessarily germinate at the site of the experience but may grow and bear fruit much later.

Defining evaluation and assessment as terms in drama

Evaluation is perhaps a more general term than assessment; the core meaning is making a judgement about someone or something. However, as Kemmis and Stake (1988, p. 9) pointed out, our judgements are always made 'in a context of understanding shaped by personal biographies, by culture and by ideology'. In a drama experience, as in any other learning context, teachers frequently make judgements about their students' responses and how involved they are in what they're doing. To a degree these judgements may feel intuitive, but, as Ben Shahn observed (Best 1980, p. 124):

> intuition in art is actually the result of prolonged tuition. The so-called innocent eye does not exist. The eye at birth cannot perceive at all, and it is only through training that it learns to recognise what it sees.

Nevertheless teachers do need to trust their 'intuitive' judgements when they're observing what students are learning through drama.

John Thompson (1991, p. 80) argues that as teachers gain experience in drama, they become *connoisseurs*, able to lead their students to the appreciation of complexity. But for this to happen, they must 'know what to look for, be able to recognise skill, form and creativity'. Then they can use their connoisseur's eye to make evaluations that will, for example, affect decisions about the pacing and direction of learning experiences. Judgements about particular experiences may also change the way they use similar experiences in another context.

Assessment is a term often used to refer to measuring performance or appraising it in some other way. However, it can present problems when applied to learning through drama. While some drama activities can be measured (e.g. a student's ability to write in role, or depict a character with a sculpted image), others are less easily assessed. For example, new understandings that develop from the exploration of ideas or emotions may not be observable for some time. A student who's explored the notion of getting old through enacting Miss Nancy in *Wilfred Gordon Macdonald Partridge* (Margaret Wild & Julie Vivas) may not be able to express his concerns in any tangible way until he has to decide on nursing home care for a parent many years later.

The most useful form of assessment for K–6 drama is **formative** rather than **summative** — that is, teachers will usually rely on day-to-day value judgements to pinpoint areas that require further development. Often the term 'assessment' is equated with a numerical mark but, as pointed out by Rowntree (cited in Thompson 1991, p. 76), assessment occurs:

> whenever one person, in some kind of interaction, direct or indirect, with another, is conscious of obtaining and interpreting information about the knowledge and understanding, or abilities and attitudes of that other person. To some extent it is an attempt to know that person.

Undoubtedly teachers and students are better served by the sort of descriptive assessment which attempts to give a detailed, complex, ongoing account of each student's learning.

Principles of evaluation and assessment in drama

- Assessment and evaluation must always acknowledge the subjective nature of the judgement being made and the purpose of the judgement. However, as adults experienced in the teaching of drama, teachers are able to apply their appreciation of the art form to their subjective judgements.
- As much information should be gathered from as many different perspectives as possible (preferably including the student's own perspective).
- Students are often very self-aware and self-evaluation strategies can be very rewarding.
- Providing opportunities to talk, draw and write about drama experiences is important.
- Not every piece of work need be assessed.
- Criteria for assessment in drama need to be developed and discussed with students, so that they understand the purpose(s) of assessment activities. For example, if you want students to show their ability to work together in small groups, criteria for demonstrating this ability need to be workshopped.
- The most important component of evaluation and assessment is the reflective component.

Appropriate evaluation tools in drama

Whole class and small group discussion
Such discussions can take place during a drama experience or afterwards. Sometimes you may decide to stop the drama at a certain point to discuss students' responses, other possibilities and so on; at other times you may find it better to wait till the end of the session. Small group discussions can sometimes be more productive than whole class ones, and you can either record these yourself or nominate a student in each group to provide a report.

Student journals
Students can use journals to reflect on their own learning and that of their peers. Comments on both sides of the spectrum can be illuminating, as these examples show:

> People were doing their own thing and not paying attention. Most of us sounded too young to be adults in the story.

> This drama made me think of people on the streets and the things that happened to them.

> The drama was a total mess. Everyone was mucking up. I tried to be in role, but I really felt upset and angry because everyone was silly.

> It was fun. It feels good when you play someone else, and get to feel how your character would feel.

Journal entries like these can redirect the focus of your teaching. For example, one Grade 5 teacher was able to adapt his lessons when he read:

> I felt bored. The hot-seating was OK, and the circle activities were fun but the rest [talking] was boring.

It was clear that he needed to build in more physical activity and give this particular student more space to express herself.

Teacher journals
You can keep your own record of your perceptions during drama sessions. Descriptive comments, follow-up suggestions and anecdotal accounts can all be included, and photos can form a really valuable supplement.

Portfolios
Each student keeps a scrapbook or folder containing photos, writing and drawing to record his or her development in drama. Responses from parents and friends can also be included.

Written and graphic responses in or out of role
The drawing of Timothy and Phillip on the raft early in *The Cay* (p. 20 above) illustrates the value of responding in visual terms. However, more conventional written responses can be equally valuable, as demonstrated in

Evaluation and assessment

Two students use a frozen moment to show their interpretation of an imagined situation. Such a photo helps to evaluate their grasp of this particular strategy as well as their understanding of the drama being played out.

these Year 5 comments on readers' theatre:

> When you read the script and act it feels that you are in the book and you feel really proud of yourself.
>
> I found readers' theatre interesting 'cos it was fun. It makes you not be so shy in front of an audience. I like when I read because it gives me a chance to use another accent. It's fun being someone else for a change.
>
> I like readers' theatre because if you want to read poems or act you have to improve how you say it.

Observation
Systematically observing a number of students each week is also worthwhile. Alternatively students can be appointed as observers, either of a group or (as critical friends) of just one peer.

Audio/video recording
Video recording can provoke discussion of particular points amongst a whole class or within small groups. Audio tapes will help students and teacher to concentrate on the aural dimension and are especially valuable for readers' theatre.

Questionnaires and rating scales
Students can be asked to respond to a series of questions, either in written form or orally. Younger students can draw their responses. Rating on a scale from a very sad to a very happy face is also feasible for younger students.

Conclusion

If drama evaluation is seen as formative, it won't become a chore or an exercise performed merely to complete a section on a student's report. Evaluation strategies are a really important facet of any teacher's planning, because they reveal student learning and the quality of the teaching. Most of the strategies described above are useful across all key learning areas. They are just as informative for students and should enable them to assume increasing responsibility for their own learning.

ENVOI

Theories about how students learn have changed radically since the mechanistic, behaviourist approaches advocated earlier this century. As Betty Jane Wagner (1995, p. 62) writes:

> Children are no longer described as Dickens' schoolmaster Gradgrind in *Hard Times* saw them — 'little vessels . . . ready to have imperial gallons of facts poured into them until they were full to the brim'. No. Now there is a widespread recognition that knowledge is not passively poured into students' heads but, instead, constructed by each learner. As learners actively engage in experiencing the world, they are just as actively constructing models in their brain to account for what they are undergoing . . . human beings do not simply soak up other persons' meaning. Rather, they actively create their own.

Sadly, however, the institution of the school hasn't yet really explored the potential of drama — or, indeed, of the other creative arts — to open up the meanings of our everyday experience, to make new connections and uncover new possibilities through the use of our imaginations.

The list of educational theorists and writers who have advocated the centrality of the imagination in the development of language, literacy, thinking and learning seems endless (Dewey, Piaget, Vygotsky, Bruner, Barnes, Britton, Rosen, Smith, Greene . . . to name only a few). In fact, Bruner (1990, p. 4) asserts that our capacity to create both in science and in narrative depends on our ability to imagine a world. Dramatic play enables us to enter imaginatively into different worlds and to explore the ambiguity and contradictions of the world we live in. Educational drama is far more than a 'box of tricks' or a fun lesson-filler, only good for providing a motivational lead into 'real' learning about what can be measured or solved. Use of the drama strategies described in this book can foster the development of our students' imaginations and help them grow in their understanding of different perspectives and meanings. It can also help them to envision potential changes and ask new questions.

But perhaps you still feel apprehensive about drama? Jodie Delofski, a beginning primary teacher, recently wrote in her journal:

> I have mixed emotions about drama. I feel apprehensive and shy and I worry that I can't think of what to say in role. I worry that I can't improvise quickly . . . at other times I'm conscious of the limited range of ideas I seem to have. I guess that this reflects a lack of experience with drama on my part. So how can I teach drama?
>
> However, I see that drama could be useful in giving students confidence, helping them to interact and giving them positive images and awareness of

their bodies . . . I can also see that using drama could be effective in integrating curriculum areas. Kids can readily construct knowledge and concepts as they construct roles and alternative worlds. Drama is one of the only subjects I can think of where kids can deal with and reflect on their emotions.

We all carry baggage from our past experiences, and many of us seem to carry more than usual from our experiences of drama. This is perhaps the most powerful reason for drama remaining so neglected in the classroom. But we can no longer afford to ignore the possibilities that dramatic processes provide across the curriculum, and the only way to overcome apprehension is to make a start, however tentative. Some of the early chapters in this book suggest ways that you might do this — beginning with movement or mime or still image, setting clear guidelines and expectations for the activities, engaging in open discussion with students about your purposes, and setting aside time for reflection afterwards. A little later you can try the ideas for literature-based drama set out by Margery Hertzberg in the Appendix. Certainly, once launched, you'll find the voyage exciting and rewarding — and so will your students!

APPENDIX

DRAMA PROGRAMS FOR NOVELS AND PICTURE BOOKS

Margery Hertzberg

This appendix provides examples of how to use drama during the reading of two books — a novel, *Onion Tears* by Diana Kidd, and a picture book, *Our Excursion* by Kate Walker and David Cox. It demonstrates how children's understanding of the drama form can be developed along with their skills in reading. The ideas presented can of course be applied to other books.

Framework defined

As these activities have been planned to enhance children's reading development, they have been designed to follow the model for reading literature developed by Nicoll, Unsworth and Parker (1987). This model was chosen because it clearly delineates the different aspects of the reading process, viz:

- getting ready for the text
- getting into the text
- coming back to the text
- going beyond the text.

Each activity appears under the appropriate category so that its purpose in terms of reading skill development is clear. Examples of responses from children are also included, in separate frames.

Diana Kidd, *Onion Tears* (Collins)

Resources   One copy of *Onion Tears*; extracts on overhead transparencies.

Suitability   Years 4–7. Note that if your class includes students with a refugee background, you should consider their own experiences before using this book as a focus for close study. They might find some of the incidents traumatic.

Synopsis   A Vietnamese refugee girl, Nam-Huong, arrives in Australia without her immediate family. She lives with an adopted 'aunt' and attends the local school, where her unwillingness to join in or talk to the other children is misunderstood. Cross-cultural differences are a major theme.

Sequence of activities The activities relate to the first section of the book, where cross-cultural differences are explored through various incidents of teasing. The purpose of this sequence is for students to react and respond to the situations portrayed in the text. It's better not to draw attention to the teasing theme initially, as it will surface naturally in the course of the activities.

Getting into the text

Reading
Read the text down to page 14.

Hot-seating
Although we don't yet know much about the characters, it's useful to hot-seat a student as Nam-Huong to explore her likely feelings at this stage of the story. It doesn't matter whether the supposed Nam-Huong's answers match the subsequent story-line. The aim is for students to predict some of the feelings and reactions which Nam-Huong might have felt, given the incidents that have occurred so far.

> *When one Year 5 student assumed the role of Nam-Huong, she was asked if she liked her teacher. She said she didn't because the teacher let Danny tease her. In fact, in the story Nam-Huong's teacher becomes her mentor and a very close relationship develops between them. However, a mistaken prediction can form the basis for a later discussion of what really happens as the story unfolds.*

Getting into the text and coming back to the text

Sculpting, still image and 'cooled' drama
Put the following extract (from page 9) onto an overhead transparency and leave it displayed throughout the activities.

> Everyone at school keeps asking me what my name means.
> 'Does it mean princess?' Mary says.
> 'COCONUT!' Tessa shouts.
> 'Butterfly!' 'Dragon!' They all try and guess.
> 'I know,' says Danny. 'It means *DIM SIM!*'
> But I just shake my head.
> One day I'll tell them what it means.
> My Mum loved my name. She said it was very special.

Sculpting Divide the students into pairs and ask one to sculpt the other to show how Nam-Huong might look as the other characters focus on her. All the sculptures can be shown as statues in the centre of the room and the class can then discuss differences and similarities.

Still image   Divide students into groups of four, in which they assume the roles of Nam-Huong, Danny, Tessa and Mary. The groups discuss the extract displayed and then make a still image of the scene using all four characters. Each group in turn shows their image to the rest of the class.

'Cooled' drama   In groups of five, students further discuss the scene and break it into three sections, each reflecting a different emotion. Each section is then frozen and held as an image, with selected dialogue added by a narrator. The narrator also signals with a hand clap when to change to the next image in the sequence. Groups practice their chosen sequence.

> *One Year 6 group did it this way:*
>
> *1st image. Mary, Tessa and Danny were all leaning forward and looking at Nam-Huong.*
> *Narrator: 'What does your name mean?' (Clap)*
>
> *2nd image. This time Mary had her arm around Nam-Huong to comfort her. Tessa was distancing herself and Danny had his hands on his hips and a spiteful expression on his face.*
> *Narrator: 'It means Dim Sim!' (Clap)*
>
> *3rd image. Nam-Huong turned away and hung her head. Mary looked concerned, Tessa looked indifferent and Danny was sniggering.*
> *(Narrator paused in silence and then clapped to signify the end)*

Coming back to the text and going beyond the text

Role walk and tapping in

Reading and discussion   Read from page 15 to page 21, and put the following extract (from page 21) onto an overhead transparency.

> *Rice and pork*
> *and funny black sauce.*
> *Whose lunch is it?*
> *Nam's lunch* (upside down)

Discuss this to elicit Danny's motive for writing it and to find out how students think Nam-Huong might be feeling.

Role walk   Ask students to close their eyes and imagine they are Nam-Huong. Then conduct a role walk with students in role as Nam-Huong. While they're walking, ask them to think of a word to describe how they feel when they read this 'poem'.

Tapping in While the role walk is in progress, tap participants on the shoulder to signal that they are to say their word. Allow them to say 'Pass' if they don't want to share their thoughts at this stage.

Going beyond the text (to come back to it)

Verbal collage

Give each student a strip of paper. Without identifying themselves, they write on it a word or phrase to describe how people might feel when teased or humiliated. Papers are then collected in the middle of the room and students each take one (but not their own). This procedure ensures the anonymity of what follows.

Arrange the group as a choir and ask one person to say their word or phrase. Others follow one at a time when they feel it's appropriate. It doesn't matter if they happen to coincide with someone else, but they shouldn't treat it as a race. The end comes when there is no one left to speak — an effective and poignant close.

If students want to repeat the collage, there's no need to keep the sequence constant; it will change spontaneously each time.

Parallel improvisation

Divide students into groups of four to five and explain that they are to improvise an incident in which someone is humiliated, bullied and/or teased. For example, it might involve a student being teased in the playground. It may help students to focus their ideas if you write these questions on the board:

Who are we?
Where are we?
What are we doing?
Why are we doing it?

Tell groups that the improvisation is to end just as the incident is about to be resolved and that the ending is to be shown as a still image. This builds in an element of constraint (see p. 8) and also ensures that the improvisation will lead somewhere instead of just fizzling out.

Suggest that improvisations last about a minute. Make sure that you allow enough time for planning (about ten minutes), as this will enable students to really explore and discuss the issues. Then encourage them to get up and rehearse, as it's in the 'doing' that most refinement occurs.

> *One Year 4 group played children being selected for softball teams by the team captains. The improvisation ended just as the last child was very reluctantly called to one of the teams. The concluding image showed four children sniggering and the unwanted child cowering.*

Viewing, reflection and debriefing

Groups take it in turns to perform their improvisations. After all have been seen, discuss the issues raised. Use questions to provoke discussion — e.g. 'You're no longer ———, but how did you feel when you were?', or 'Did you like the character you were?'

From improvisation to playbuilding

It's often possible to extend the improvisations to make a play. Students need to reconsider them and work out a suitable sequence for combining them (which could be interspersed with the voice collage worked on previously).

> *One Year 6 class performed six different improvisations that ranged from bullying incidents in the playground to teasing a poor reader and sibling rivalry. Two were similar and were folded into one. The class decided to have a narrator, who introduced the play with a short account of teasing and its consequences (written by the whole class). Then the rest of the class (who were seated in position) stood up and performed the first of three voice collages. They sat down again while the first two improvisations were played. The voice collage was repeated (in a different form) and then came the remaining three improvisations. To conclude, the voice collage was repeated once more, but this time each student left the stage after speaking.*

Possible extension: playing to an external audience

If, for example, it's your turn to provide the assembly item, the play can be quite quickly refined and rehearsed for an external audience.

Kate Walker & David Cox, *Our Excursion* (Omnibus)

Resources   At least eight copies of *Our Excursion*.

Suitability   Years 2–6. The language is simple, but the main theme (consequences when people act at cross purposes) appeals to a wide age range. This book is particularly suitable for upper primary students who are reluctant readers and for ESL students who need special assistance with English.

Synopsis   *Our Excursion* is a picture book story. The school excursion to the Art Gallery begins ordinarily enough, but a series of humorous mishaps results in the unfolding of extraordinary events.

Point of view and narrative style   One objective of this drama program is to enhance students' understanding of point of view and narrative style. The events are related in the style of a recount by one of the children, but there is an absence of descriptive language and detail. However, the illustrations extend the story, revealing much that's not found in the written text.

Getting ready for the text

Prediction
By looking at the cover students can predict that this book is about a class of happy children who go on an excursion by public transport (the illustration is framed within a tram ticket).

Getting into the text

First reading
Read the book with your students. Multiple copies are vital because a complete reading is only possible when both written and visual texts are available.

Coming back to the text

Second reading
A second reading is important because many aspects can only be understood once the first reading is completed. For example, there must be some discussion of narrator and point of view, and it's not clear till the end that the narrator is one of the girls. Discuss also how the illustrations provide details missing from the written text. For example, although Roberto is a major character, his exploits are only fully realised in the illustrations.

Hot-seating
A significant and commendable feature of *Our Excursion* is the portrayal of individual characters. However, it's only possible to appreciate this after several readings. Children are quick to notice that one of the boys, Dennis, is to be seen picking his nose in each illustration, and you can turn this into a useful focus for looking at what distinguishes the other characters. However, if you want to avoid concentration on Dennis, you can write on the board the names of the major characters (Ms Mobbs, Roberto, 'Me', Carmel, Ann, Jane and the ice-cream man) and ask students to select one to examine in more depth.

Students have to refer back to relevant sections of the book to explore their chosen character, and then, as a whole class activity, they can hot-seat each other to develop a fuller profile of the various characters.

Sculpting
There are quite a number of dramatic moments in *Our Excursion* which are suitable for sculpting, but again they're only apparent when text and illustrations are matched. One possibility would be to divide the class into pairs and have one partner sculpt the other as Carmel when her lunch box is dropped onto the road.

Reflection and discussion

As students examine the sculptures, focus discussion on the use of body language to interpret a situation.

Still image

The tension arising from a complication in a story can be 'felt' more acutely when students make a still image. For example, they might choose the moment when the ice-cream man demands payment but the children have no money. Have them form groups of six, refer back to the picture and decide on the role each will take. Then they arrange and position themselves to capture the moment.

Reflection and discussion

Again, discuss how meaning is conveyed by using expression, gesture and position.

Tapping in

Select one of the images and ask the group to form it again. Tap each participant on the shoulder in turn, so that they verbalise the thoughts of their character in this situation.

> *In the book Jane and Ann are always portrayed as 'good' children. In this particular illustration they are seen enjoying their ice-creams. In her role as Jane, one Year 3 student said, 'I know this is wrong but I'm going to eat it anyway!'*

Summary

Up to this point, dramatic strategies have been used to achieve a detailed reading of the book. However, there's been no drama as such. The remainder of the unit uses *Our Excursion* as a stimulus for playbuilding, at the same time drawing attention to its linguistic and visual structures, which are typical of many modern picture books.

Going beyond the text

Explanation

Refer back to the book, reiterating that it is a recount written from one girl's point of view, and propose that the class develop a drama based on a fictional excursion in which unforeseen events occur. The overall framework is to be planned by the whole class; then groups of six will each plan one of the scenes and develop an unscripted improvisation lasting about two minutes.

A script in the style of a recount will be jointly constructed and interspersed between each improvisation. This text will perform the function of the narrator in *Our Excursion*, while the improvisations will reflect the illustrations.

Defining the drama

Write the following headings across the board:

> WHO ARE WE?   WHERE ARE WE?
> WHAT ARE WE DOING? WHY ARE WE DOING IT?

Brainstorm and record ideas for scenarios under them (usually three are enough). Negotiate the most popular and then discuss and amplify it.

> *One Year 3 class made the following suggestions in their initial brainstorm:*
> - *Year 6 going to England to see the Queen for fun*
> - *Year 4 going on an excursion to the local area as part of a project on the local community*
> - *Year 4 going to the beach to learn about life in rock pools for a science project.*
>
> *The third proved the most popular. Further brainstorming established that the children lived in western Sydney and were going to Long Reef Beach because it had many rock pools.*

Building belief

The whole class draws a map of the setting where the drama is to take place, adding details as they occur. Although this can be done on the board, a piece of butcher's paper long enough for everyone to sit round is better, since it's easier to keep for reference in subsequent sessions.

Being involved in constructing the setting promotes a sense of ownership in the students. As the map progresses, it will clarify and extend the decisions made earlier and help to develop ideas for events that might be included in the drama.

> *Our Year 3 class decided that their drama would take place at the beach and nearby park (the travel element would be excluded), and so their map detailed this setting only. It included the rock pools, sharks and swimmers in the surf, play equipment in the park, and so forth.*

Improvisation

The class divides into groups of six, each of which selects a time and a place on the map where its improvisation will take place. At this stage groups may wish to add more details to their particular site on the map.

Planning Each group chooses an unforeseen problem. To establish the problem, groups need to make decisions about the following questions (which should be written up on the board):

What is happening?
Who is involved?
What is going to happen? (i.e. problem/tension)
How is this event going to be resolved?

Developing tension Include the constraint that the improvisation should end just as the problem occurs. It's also important to stress that as each improvisation is part of a sequence, the problem has to be one that allows the story to continue. For instance, no one may die!

> *One of the Year 3 groups decided their improvisation would take place on a rock platform. One of the characters was taking a photo of the group. To fit them all in, she stepped back, and back, and back . . . and the improvisation ended just as she was about to fall into another rock pool.*

Defining the focus (language, movement, mood) Ask each group to begin and end their improvisation with a still image.

Rehearsal Groups practice their improvisations.

Viewing, reflection and debriefing
Discuss the improvisations, and refine them if necessary to perfect the sequence. Reflection and debriefing are really important at this stage. As mentioned earlier, a major theme of *Our Excursion* is the consequences that result from people acting at cross purposes. Ask questions to elicit discussion about this, and how students felt in their particular roles.

Coming back to the text to go beyond the text

Writing the recount
Reiterate that the book is a recount. Re-read it and discuss the features and purposes of both written and visual texts. Then jointly construct a recount to link the improvisations.

> *The narrator's script composed by our Year 3 class began like this:*
>
> Last week our class 3B went on an excursion to Long Reef Beach. We took our clipboards and lunch. Mr Brown said we could wear our ordinary clothes but to make sure they were old ones. Some of us even brought our cameras. When we got there we had recess and then he told us to go to the toilet.

> *(Improvisation 1. This showed a child locked in the toilet and Mr Brown climbing over the door to help her out.)*
>
> *After that we went over to the rock pools. We had to sketch and label the animals and plants we could see. If we had a camera we were allowed to take photos.*
>
> *(Improvisation 2. This showed a child trying to catch a crab and getting bitten on the finger.)*

Perform the sequence

In this sequence it's the process rather than the product that's of prime significance. However, with very few rehearsals the drama could be refined and performed for an external audience.

SELECT BIBLIOGRAPHY

Abbs, P. 1987, *Living Powers*, Falmer Press, London.
—— 1994, *The Educational Imperative*, Falmer Press, London.
Apple, M. 1990, *Ideology and Curriculum*, 2nd edn, Routledge, New York.
Aylwin, T. 1988, 'Telling and retelling', in *Storytelling*, Inner London Education Authority, London.
Baker, A. & Greene, E. 1977, *Storytelling: Art and Technique*, Bowker Co, New York.
Bernstein, B. 1990, *The Structure of Pedagogic Discourse: Class, Codes and Control*, vol. 4, Routledge, London.
Best, D. 1979, *The Rationality of Feeling*, Falmer Press, London.
—— 1980, 'The objectivity of artistic appreciation', *British Journal of Aesthetics*, vol. 20, no. 2.
—— 1985, *Feeling and Reason in the Arts*, Allen & Unwin, London.
Boal, A. 1992, *Theatre of the Oppressed*, Pluto Press, London.
Bolton, G. 1979, *Towards a Theory of Drama in Education*, Longman, London.
—— 1984, *Drama as Education*, Longman, London.
—— 1987, 'Drama as art', Paper presented at the British Council course, 'How do you train a drama leader?', Durham.
—— 1988, 'Drama as art', *Drama Broadsheet*, vol. 5, no. 3.
—— 1992, *New Perspectives on Classroom Drama*, Simon & Schuster, London.
Boomer, G. 1983, *Negotiating the Curriculum*, Ashton Scholastic, Sydney.
Bruner, J. 1986, *Actual Minds, Possible Worlds*, Harvard University Press, Cambridge, Mass.
—— 1996, *The Culture of Education*, Harvard University Press, Cambridge, Mass.
Burton, B. 1991, *The Act of Learning*, Longman Cheshire, Melbourne.
Byron, K. 1986, *Drama in the English Classroom*, Methuen, London.
—— & Griffin, D. 1984, 'Still image', *National Association for Drama in Education*, vol. 8.
Charters, J. & Gately, A. 1986, *Drama Anytime*, Primary English Teaching Association, Sydney.
Colwell, F. 1991, *Storytelling*, Thimble Press, Stroud, Glos.
Connolly, M. & Clandinnen, J. 1990, 'Stories of experience and narrative enquiry', *Educational Researcher*, vol. 19, no. 5.
Cremin, M. & Jones, S. 1997, 'An inquiry into the use of imagination in classroom drama with primary school children', Paper presented at the Annual Conference of the British Educational Research Association, York.
Curriculum Corporation 1994, *A Statement on the Arts for Australian Schools*, Curriculum Corporation, Melbourne.

Cusworth R. 1991, 'Using reader's theatre to explore text form', in F. McKay (ed.), *Public and Private Lessons*, Australian Reading Association, Melbourne.

—— 1995, 'The framing of educational knowledge through newstime in K–2 classrooms', PhD thesis, University of Sydney.

Darvall, L. 1992, *Drama and Curriculum*, Deakin University Press, Geelong.

Davis, D. & Lawrence, C. (eds) 1986, *Gavin Bolton: Selected Writings on Drama in Education*, Longman, London.

Egan, K. 1987, *Teaching as Storytelling*, Althouse, London, Ontario.

Erickson, S. 1990, 'Picture theatre in the classroom: a brief introduction to elements of Augusto Boal from the perspective of the drama teacher', *National Association for Drama in Education*, vol. 14.

Finn, B. (chair) 1991, *Young People's Participation in Post-Compulsory Education and Training*, Report of the Australian Education Council Review Committee, AGPS, Canberra.

Fleming, M. 1994, *Starting Drama Teaching*, David Fulton, London.

Flournoy, V. 1990, *The Patchwork Quilt*, Puffin, London.

Fox, C. 1983, 'Talking like a book', in M. Meek (ed.), *Opening Moves*, Bedford Way Papers, no. 17, University of London, London.

—— 1993, *At the Very Edge of the Forest*, Cassell, London.

Freire, P. 1972, *Pedagogy of the Oppressed*, Sheed & Ward, London.

French, R. & French, J. 1991, *Puppet Drama*, Anzea, Sydney.

Gardner, H. 1993, *The Arts and Human Development*, Basic Books, New York.

Giacomelli, D. 1994, 'Values and evaluation in drama', *Journal of the Educational Drama Association*, vol. 2, no. 1.

Greene, M. 1995, *Releasing the Imagination*, Jossey Bass, San Francisco.

Hardy, B. 1975, *Tellers and Listeners*, Athlone Press, London.

Hargreaves, D. 1990, *Children and the Arts*, Open University Press, Milton Keynes.

Haseman, B. & O'Toole, J. 1987, *Dramawise*, Heinemann, Melbourne.

Heathcote, D. 1988, *Drama and Social Change: Dorothy Heathcote 1984 New Zealand Lectures*, Kohia Teachers Centre, NZ.

—— & Bolton, G. 1994, *Drama for Learning: An Account of Heathcote's Mantle of the Expert*, Heinemann, Portsmouth, NH.

Hertzberg, M. 1996, 'Using drama in literature-based reading programs', *The Primary Educator*, vol. 2, no. 5.

Hodgson, J. & Richards, E. 1972, 'Drama as synthesis', in J. Hodgson (ed.), *The Uses of Drama*, Methuen, London.

Hornbrook, D. 1989, *Education and Dramatic Art*, Blackwell, Oxford.

—— 1991, *Education in Drama: Casting the Dramatic Curriculum*, Falmer Press, London.

Hughes, J. (ed.) 1991, *Drama in Education: The State of the Art*, Educational Drama Association, Sydney.

Johnson, L. & O'Neill, C. (eds) 1984, *Dorothy Heathcote: Collected Writings on Education and Drama*, Hutchinson, London.

Select bibliography

Johnstone, K. 1981, *Impro: Improvisation and the Theatre*, Methuen, London.
Keller, B. 1991, *Puppy Love*, unpublished TS, Toetruck Theatre, Sydney.
Kemmis, S. & Stake, R. 1988, *Evaluating Curriculum*, Deakin University Press, Geelong.
Kempe, A. & Holroyde, R. 1994, *Imaging Series*, Hodder & Stoughton, London.
Kress, G. 1986, *Linguistic Processes in Sociocultural Practice*, Deakin University Press, Geelong.
Langer, S. 1953, *Feeling and Form*, Routledge & Kegan Paul, London.
Loeschke, M. 1982, *All about Mime: Understanding and Exploring the Expressive Silence*, Prentice Hall, New Jersey.
Martin, J. & Rothery, J. 1982, *Writing Project Report*, Working Papers in Linguistics, no. 2, University of Sydney, Sydney.
Matthews, S. 1988, *Getting into the Act*, GP Books, NZ.
Mayer, E. (chair) 1992, *Employment-Related Key Competencies: A Proposal for Consultation*, Owen King, Melbourne.
Metropolitan West Region, NSW 1984, *Playbuilding*, Government Printer, Sydney.
Moore, P. 1988, *When Are We Going To Have More Drama?*, Nelson, Sydney.
Morgan, N. & Saxton, J. 1987, *Teaching Drama: A Mind of Many Wonders*, Hutchinson, London.
—— 1994, *Asking Better Questions*, Pembroke, Markham, Ontario.
Morris, M. 1993, *Boss of the Pool: Adapted for the Stage*, Currency Press, Sydney.
Neelands, J. 1984, *Making Sense of Drama*, Heinemann, London.
—— 1990, *Structuring Drama Work*, Cambridge University Press, Cambridge.
New London Group 1996, 'Pedagogy of multiliteracies: designing social futures', *Harvard Educational Review*, vol. 66, no. 1.
Newland, A. 1988, 'This is your life', in *Storytelling*, Inner London Education Authority, London.
Nicoll, V., Unsworth, L. & Parker, R. 1987, *Dimensions*, Nelson, Melbourne.
Nixon, J. (ed.) 1982, *Drama and the Whole Curriculum*, Hutchinson, London.
—— 1987, *Teaching Drama: A Teaching Skills Workbook*, Macmillan, London.
NSW Board of Studies 1994, *Creative Arts Writing Brief*, Board of Studies NSW, Sydney.
O'Neill, C. 1983, 'Context or essence: the place of drama in the curriculum', in C. Day & J. Norman (eds), *Issues in Educational Drama*, Falmer Press, London.
—— 1995, *Drama Worlds: A Framework for Process Drama*, Heinemann, London.
—— et al. 1976, *Drama Guidelines*, Heinemann, London.
—— & Lambert, A. 1982, *Drama Structures*, Hutchinson, London.
O'Toole, J. 1992, *The Process of Drama*, Routledge, London.
Queensland Department of Education 1991, *Years 1–10 Drama Curriculum Guidelines*, Education Department of Queensland, Brisbane.
—— 1994, *Drama Makes Meaning*, Education Department of Queensland, Brisbane.

Robertson, M. 1990, *True wizardry: readers theatre in the classroom*, PEN 79, Primary English Teaching Association, Sydney.

Robinson, K. 1980, *Exploring Theatre and Education*, Heinemann, London.

Rosen, H. (n.d.), *Stories and Meanings*, National Association for the Teaching of English, London.

Rosenblatt, L. 1978, *The Reader, the Text, the Poem: A Transactional Theory of Literary Work*, Southern Illinois University Press, Carbondale, IL.

Ross, M. (ed.) 1982, *The Development of Aesthetic Experience*, Pergamon Press, Oxford.

Schon, D. 1987, *Educating the Reflective Practitioner*, Jossey Bass, San Francisco.

Simons, J. 1991, 'Concept development and drama: scaffolding the learning', in J. Hughes (ed.), *Drama in Education: The State of the Art*, Educational Drama Association, Sydney.

—— 1997, 'Drama pedagogy and the art of double meaning', *Research in Drama Education Journal*, vol. 2, no. 2.

Slade, P. 1954, *Child Drama*, University of London Press, London.

Smith, F. 1992, *To Think*, Routledge, London.

South Australian Education Department 1991, *Images of Life*, Education Curriculum Studies Association, Adelaide.

Spady, B. 1992, *Outcomes-Based Education*, Australian Curriculum Studies, Belconnen, ACT.

Stein, M. 1971, 'Creativity as intra- and interpersonal process', in R. Holsinger, C. Jordan & L. Levenson, *The Creative Encounter*, Scott Foresman, Glenview, IL.

Thompson, J. 1991, 'Assessing drama: allowing for meaningful interpretation', in J. Hughes (ed.), *Drama in Education: The State of the Art*, Educational Drama Association, Sydney.

Vygotsky, L. 1976, *Thought and Language*, MIT Press, Cambridge, Mass.

Wagner, B. 1976, *Dorothy Heathcote: Drama as a Learning Medium*, National Education Association, Washington DC.

—— 1995, 'A theoretical framework for improvisational drama', *National Association for Drama in Education*, vol. 19, no. 2.

Warren, K. 1991, 'Drama for young children', in J. Hughes (ed.), *Drama in Education: The State of the Art*, Educational Drama Association, Sydney.

—— 1993, *Hooked on Drama*, Macquarie University Institute of Early Childhood, Sydney.

Way, B. 1967, *Development through Drama*, Longman, London.

Wilson, C. 1994, 'Drama as a teaching technique to increase motivation in learning', *Journal of the Educational Drama Association*, vol. 2, no. 1.

Winner, E. 1982, *Invented Worlds: Psychology of the Arts*, Harvard University Press, Cambridge, Mass.

Witkin, R. 1976, *The Intelligence of Feeling*, Heinemann, London.

Woodward, H. 1993, *Negotiated Evaluation*, Primary English Teaching Association, Sydney.